I was visiting Biddie, one of my oldest and most favourite patients in her nursing home locally. She was formally as bright as a button, but over the last few years had slowly succumbed to Alzheimer's disease. She had known me well for many years, and we had always had a good rapport, but I had heard that latterly she was not even recognising some close friends. "Hello Biddie" I said hopefully, "you know who I am don't you?" "No", she said. "Come on Biddie, you remember all those times I have been to see you, we had lots of lovely conversation together. Are you really sure you don't know who I am?" "NO" she grunted. "Really, Biddie, look at me and see if you can remember who I am". An air of resignation came over her and she considered the question for a moment. I thought the penny had dropped. "No, I don't know who you are, but that lady over there, she is called Sister, and if you go and ask her, she will tell you who you are"!

It was incidents like that which make me look back on my career in Medicine with so many fond recollections.

I'm not sure how it started, but it has all gone so quickly. One minute I was a nipper in Balham in South London, and now I am in the depths of France leading a life of leisure, a grey haired old bugger drinking wine and getting ready for the next dance class. So what was in between?

I have had a lovely career, engendered by a comfortable family and good luck rather than any talent for direction. From the Battersea Grammar school, where career guidance was non- existent, to ending up at Medical School and then a varied path ending with thirty years practise in deepest Dorset. It may all have been so different if the primary school teacher in Balham had not been so strict with us and made me pass the eleven plus exam. It may have been so different if I had not done well in the sciences at O level and been made to do them at A level. It may have been different if my pal did not apply to Medical School, and suggest I did the same thing. But such is life, and medicine has been a real education in the ways of others, from all walks of life and from all social strata's. We are all the same with our pants off, and social barriers wither away in the presence of a medical man. I have had the pleasure to work with many different races, and will remain convinced that we are all basically the same emotionally when stripped of all our cultural restraints.

My time has been illuminated by numerous amusing events which I am attempting to recall here. Most are still fresh in my mind, some may have been embroidered slightly, but the great majority are the daily trials, tribulations and funny moments of the Medical Man. I really can't stand hearing whinging doctors, we have such a well paid and privileged position, and especially nowadays, the hours are less than many other workers. The problem is that most doctors have not had another job.

MEDICAL SCHOOL.

In the mid-sixties simple passes at three A levels was enough to get into the London Medical Schools. They had to be the sciences, of course, but very few pupils gained A grades in those days. My three B's would probably only have got me into Tesco's today. Instead great value was placed on the interview, and I really cocked up my first at Kings College. Having arrived in the nick of time after my old Vespa scooter had broken down, and with hands covered in dirty grease, I was asked my opinion of the then recent hooliganism between the Mods and Rockers at Clacton beach. Being a South London Mod at the time (with weekly attendance at the Streatham Locarno), my reaction was that lots of my mates were there but my scooter was broken I and I couldn't attend! There was lots of coughing and spluttering and the combined look of the interviewing body relayed my inevitable failure!

Charing Cross Hospital Medical School recognised the latent talent within the crude exterior however, and the first meeting with fellow students, only about thirty in the year, was one of bewilderment. With my strong local accent it was very difficult to understand some of the other chaps, especially the Welshman from the valleys who I am sure was speaking another language. And the beautifully spoken ladies from Public Schools, who seemed so refined and cool. The teenage hormones were at full flow in those days, and I remember being slightly disappointed by the female talent on display, but hospitals are full of nurses, and the thought comforted me enormously. It was a new world I was entering, full of hidden promises and lots of sport, and maybe even some studying.

Yes, we did have to study. None of this three lectures a week nonsense, but full daily education from morning to late afternoon. All the men had to wear a tie and jacket, and ladies were forbidden to wear trousers. Yes I know it sounds Dickensian, but this was in 1966! The usual harsh introduction into the profession included cutting up dead bodies and attending grisly post mortems. The mortuary technician was elderly and had a wooden leg, and his thumping footsteps and the smell of the chemicals were horrible, but only one girl fainted. All learning had to be done from textbooks, the computer had not been invented, and they cost lots of cash. The School head porter, Old Bill, was a tall, languid, chain smoking Irishman who had seen it all and done it all for years. He sold books from his little nicotine smelling office, which he had acquired, sometimes legally, but often tomes he had found in the premises. A couple of years into the course he tried to sell me an anatomy book that I had "lost" a year previously!

The social life and the sport were wonderful. For a London wise teenager to be able to meet so many different fellow students and nurses it was more than academic education. It is true that we tended to stay mainly in a medical environment, but who needed anything else when all appetites were satisfied? The School building was, as the name suggests, in the centre of London, adjacent to Trafalgar Square. It was dark, scruffy, and was demolished many years ago, and the adjacent Hospital is now a Police Station. I well remember pushing a hospital bed to a local theatre for our annual pantomime review, aided by some nurses in uniform, around Trafalgar Square in rush hour. The traffic all stopped for us and even the Police waved us through without question. Not possible now! Sport was only allowed on a Wednesday afternoon, but the break during an otherwise full week was always a highlight. Soccer, Rugby, Cricket and golf were the main pursuits, but the odd game of mixed tennis was available on the beautiful playing field in the depths of Surrey. Sharing flats with other students was an education in itself, highlights being the numerous parties we held, although my recollection of many is veiled by consumption of Watneys' Party Ten cans. I do remember well my flatmate being Rugby captain and having to wash all our jerseys, frequently in our bath! Washing up was also not a popular pastime, and another flatmate once bought some bleach to stop the smell rather than doing the chores! They were happy but really busy times, as the learning required was intense and unrelenting, with frequent examinations, both oral and written. The former often involved pathology, and finals produced a couple of worthy incidents.

One Irish student was red headed, confident and stroppy. He was also clever, which was a bit unfair, and usually sailed through his exams. One pathology lecturer did not like his overconfidence and was determined to bring him down a peg or two. During one important test, he was handed a pot containing a pathological specimen he did not recognise, and was questioned aggressively about it. The exam was in one of the local high rise buildings with views over the Strand. "You obviously have no idea what this is or what you are talking about. Do you know how many students I have failed today with this specimen" Paddy lost his cool. Big time. "No, I don't know how many feckin' students you have failed today but I am the last feckin' student you are going to fail with this feckin' pot". He grabbed the specimen, stood up, and threw it out of the open window down onto the street below. I believe he is now a minister of Health in Ireland.

But not all examiners are aggressive, some just like to have fun. One of my year mates was a tall, elegant and very reserved lady. She was also very bright, and knew all the books by heart. Again the examination was in Pathology and she was given a pot containing a testicle. The examiner began his questioning very gently, and asked all about the functions of the organ. She was completely informed and imparted the correct answers with ease. She was then asked why the testicles are found on the outside of the body rather than on the inside. Knowing that temperature control is important to sperm maturation, and that conditions need to be cooler than the rest of the body, she gave a good explanation. "And is that true for all mammals?" she was asked. Now we don't do other animals on the course, and this was a bit outside her range of knowledge. She became much less assured. "Yes, I think so" she said, clearly unsure of herself now. "And what about the whale, is that a mammal?" Heart racing, and knowing she was about to reach the end of her resources she replied "Yes, Sir, it is." The dread of a first time failure in an exam loomed ahead. "And why does the whale not have its testicles hanging outside its body, tell me that" A pause, the student becoming red in the face and visibly perspiring, most unusual for this confident female. "Come on girl, you must know the answer" "I'm very sorry, Sir, but I don't know" Another pause, longer this time. "Because of the sharks you stupid girl!"

Before the drink driving laws came about, studies had to be done to find the level of alcohol in the bloodstream that causes performance to suffer. After one lecture we were addressed by a senior officer from the Police at New Scotland Yard, a mile or two away from the college. He was looking for volunteers to come to the Yard, spend the day there, drink various alcoholic potions and have blood taken for research. The stampede of offers was modified by this taking place on a Wednesday, when lots of us played rugby, but several of my fellows were accepted and duly attended. All went well to begin with, the drinks were drunk, lots of silly games were played, and songs sung. Bear in mind that this was really drinking to oblivion, all completely within the law, and a possibly unique situation. By mid- afternoon, inhibitions had evaporated. Some of us become aggressive with alcohol, some amorous, and some sleepy. And some try to escape! One of our number, now a very eminent Professor, managed to evade the guarding officers, some of whom were engaged in the singing, and made his way out of New Scotland Yard via an emergency exit. He was well known for his extreme antics when intoxicated, and this information was relayed by his drunken mates to the now concerned officers. The thought of a major incident caused by a blameless student deliberately intoxicated by the Police Force obviously promoted an immediate alert. Police all over central London were asked to track down this potential villain, but to apprehend him with all due gentleness in view of the circumstances involved. Luckily he was found snoring next to some dustbins behind Victoria Station. He still can't remember that afternoon!

I have always enjoyed working with the Police, but sometimes fellow students have been less kind. A well-known incident some years ago involved a student removing the defining part of a male's anatomy for a Rag Day stunt. The organ was preserved in formalin, then sewn into the fly of the chap's trousers, covered by an overcoat. As the day progressed, the organ was exposed in a crowded London street, and, after complaints by the public, the perpetrator was about to be arrested by a Police Officer. At the moment of arrest, a large pair of scissors was produced, and the organ amputated. The Officer fainted and the escape was made!

Medical training involves lots of practical work. To begin with it involved anatomy dissections and laboratory experiments, but after the first couple of years we began to get involved in the Hospital proper. There were so many practical skills to master. At this stage we worked in small groups, usually about half a dozen or so, and had to attend outpatient clinics and various operations. I remember well the first glimpse I had of the contents of an open abdomen. The problem was that at that time I needed to wear glasses due to short sight. A new pair had just been received, but they were a bit large for my nose. Wearing a mask and gloves for the first time and wary of not touching anything, I was instructed to lean over and identify the gall bladder. I could feel my glasses slipping gradually down my nose. Next stop into the gaping void of guts! I don't know how I managed, but the abdomen did not receive an unwelcome foreign body, and I now wear contact lenses.

Our firm, as the small groups were called, was all male, very testosterone fuelled and great fun. The senior tutors were often from the nursing staff and very used to teaching young males. Obstetrics was fun, with a range of midwives, all hugely experienced and in complete command of us young whippersnappers. I have even given birth! We all had to lie on the ground in a circle around out tutor, holding our legs up and panting. Most of us were in the Rugby team, and all I could think about was what our opponents would think of our display. I never fancied Obstetrics as a career, but enjoyed delivering babies In General Practise. And I did admire one of the Consultants, who reckoned he could tell the sex of a baby by putting his hand on the patients' abdomen. He was right half the time, but when accused of making a mistake he would produce his diary, where he had written the opposite sex on the day of his prediction, and show it to the impressed mother. That was only for Private Patient of course.

Sigmoidoscopy involved looking into the rear end of the bowel. In our day it was done via a rigid tube, about 2cm in diameter and about 40cm long. The end had a bulb to light the way, and because the bowel tends to collapse around the end of the tube, a puffer was provided to introduce air and push the intestine out of the way. We six were in outpatients one day, generally trying to look interested, but really admiring the new outpatient nurse who was in attendance. A patient was introduced and the procedure explained to him in detail. To our surprise the surgeon asked who had performed a sigmoidoscopy before. Thinking that claiming competence would mean a colleague would have to be involved, I said I had done several in the past-a complete lie of course." Right then, you can show us how it is done"! Bugger, I had not even seen a sigmoidoscope before, and my chums new it and started to chuckle silently. Even the pretty nurse seemed to snigger. I did know that the pump was for air, and I did know which orifice the instrument was intended for. (It is much easier in a male, less choice!). I tried to be as gentle as I could, and pumped the air in as the instrument found its way into the hidden depths. More air, I thought, as progress was interrupted. I didn't really know what I was looking for, but it must be there somewhere, perhaps higher up, more air more air. A groan came from somewhere, possibly the patient, or more likely his pressurised bowel. Suddenly the inevitable happened, an uncontrollable blowback, unfortunately not only of air, but also of watery stools. The couch was covered, the instrument blocked, and the surplus all over my arms. Luckily my face had escaped the effluent, but the snigger of colleagues now burst into uncontrollable belly laughs. Even the patient was amused and apologised as if it was his fault! The outpatients department had collapsible walls to vary to size of the rooms, and the pretty nurse and my chums were leaning against one of them. The uncontrollable laughter resulted in the wall collapsing and they were soon making a backward entrance into the adjoining suite! I can now do sigmoidoscopies.

Cash was always a bit of a problem in the early days. I was on a good student grant, not repayable in those days, but we were always looking for opportunities to make a few bob. The Bacteriology department was doing a study on the effect of antibiotics on the flora of the bowel. They wanted volunteers to provide stool samples after, and before, taking various antibiotics. The then princely sum of 1£ was to be paid for each sample daily. We enrolled immediately. Plastic bags were provided for sample collection, and they had to be presented each morning to the department. There was one slight hitch though. Samples had to be very fresh, within several minutes of delivery, and freshness was tested by temperature. We lived several miles away, and any sample would be cool on delivery. No problem. We collected our samples at home, came into the hospital half an hour early, and heated them on the radiators in the student bar. I still feel guilty that we may have spoiled some important research.

There were always lots of parties to be attended. As long a one brought a big can of beer, entry was always granted, and all the usual student activities were accounted for. It is not always easy to appear suave and experienced, as one used to attempt to be. I remember very well chatting to a lovely dark slim girl in a dim room one evening, and during the conversation, which was going rather smoothly, reaching out for a handful of the peanuts I had seen on a nearby table. After throwing back a good handful into my mouth, the realisation that I had chosen the ash tray by mistake put a sudden end to my seduction attempt. It is difficult to look attractive with a mouth full of dog ends.

We often had to live in the Hospital for a few days at a time to be on duty for the wards. Things were very different then, and having befriended the nurses, it was often possible to go to a ward, especially at night, chat up the staff and they would cook bacon and eggs from the ward kitchen for us. On special occasions we could even pinch a bottle of Mackeson Stout, which was kept to promote the appetite! We lodged in the uppermost rooms of the hospital, which is now a huge Police Station, in a group of rooms known as the stables. It had a comfortable sitting room with a large television where we would sit and watch the Cricket test matches in between our not too arduous duties. One day a chap in a brown work coat arrived and explained to us all that the rental had not been paid and he was taking the television away. We protested, of course, but respected that bills have to be paid, even by the hospital. We only found out a fortnight later that he was a local thief who had performed the same stunt in several other common rooms locally.

Some of the Consultants were fun, others too grand. One surgeon in particular, who always had the biggest and best car, used to tell us how he was fed up with having too much private operating to do and so put his fees up by ten times the original. To his astonishment his popularity, as being the obviously best surgeon because he charged so much, increased even more!

One eminent Physician was a very extrovert character. His flamboyant throwing about of his limbs when talking enthusiastically to us made us sometimes question his sanity. He did acknowledge this himself, and told a lovely story of having to take a disturbed mental patient in the back of an ambulance to Banstead Hospital, at that time famous for treating mental illness. When they arrived at the Hospital, the doctor behaved in his normally strange and almost hysterical manner in explaining about his patient's problems. At that moment, the patient himself calmly explained that he himself was in fact the doctor, and apologised for the deluded behaviour of his companion. It apparently took several hours to settle the situation!

I was enjoying the student life enormously, with no real responsibilities and a great social life. It was almost five years since I left school and the time had changed me, some things for the better. I had more confidence and looked forward to becoming a proper adult with a proper job. Old friends from school had long since left education and were earning lots of money and had flash cars and were even buying houses. On reflection I had more cash than most of my student friends because I had committed to the R.A.F. for a Short Service Commission whilst half way through the course. This meant I was independent financially from my parents, which was important to me. It also meant I could get rid of my first car, an old Ford Popular, and buy and MGA. The former cost £25 and the first repair I had to perform was to buy a roll on Lino to patch up the bodywork. Gaping holes in the wings meant all the cold air outside came into the car, and there was no heater, so blankets to wrap around the legs were the next essential. Having a car was a great advantage with the women in my life, but not always. My first Ball, at Guys Hospital, involved collecting my date, a very attractive student nurse who I was keen to impress, from her nursing home. I was wearing a Dinner Jacket for the first time and had spent as much time getting ready as I guess she had done. All was well in the old car until it started to rain. The windscreen wipers did not work, and I always carried an old potato, cut in half, to smear over the screen, and old trick which makes vision possible. It meant getting out of the car, however, and a little bit damp. That was nothing compared to the constant drip of water coming into the car on the drivers' side, directly over my left, throttle leg. I couldn't move the limb and remember clearly the ascending dampness in the trouser leg, which, by the time we had traversed London, had reached my groin. The lady, I am pleased to say, was still nice and snug under her blanket. It was difficult to look suave and confident with one leg dripping water all the way to the ballroom!

The MGA was a great improvement, both in reliability and in improving my social life. On one occasion my chum and I had been on duty as students overnight and were both tired and grumpy. We picked up my girlfriend on the way to our flat, which was a bit of a squeeze with her sitting on his lap in a two seater car. I wasn't driving too well, and another car coming the other way flashed his lights at us. I gave the usual aggressive V sign in return, only to be told that it had been a Police car! Driving dangerously in an overloaded car in which the MOT was dodgy would not go down well. I thought about driving as fast as I could to get away, but it was fruitless, as the Police drew alongside and beckoned us to stop. I did not have my licence or insurance, and the notebook came out. But then the miracle, we were asked where we had come from and explained we had all been on duty at Fulham Hospital, where the girlfriend, still in her nurses' uniform, also worked. The two burly and formerly menacing officers suddenly changed. "We had coffee and biscuits with the staff in casualty there last night, off you go"! I count myself very lucky and do not do V signs to oncoming cars any more.

Later still, the car was improved to an MGB, and on a rare holiday I decided to take a lady friend to Scotland. As a ten year old at school in London we had been taken on a trip to Loch Fyne in Argyllshire. I remember the trip vividly, as to begin with my parents explained that they could not afford the £12 the trip would cost, but my elder sister, who had started work, offered to pay £3 and the adventure was on. I had not been further than the Isle of Wight before, and Scotland was a complete unknown. We stayed in a rough part of Glasgow overnight and then on to the old converted castle at Minard the next day. The week was a complete joy to me, the wilderness of the land and the games we all played together. As an adult I was determined to go back, and this was the opportunity. We eventually arrived at what was now a rather posh hotel, obviously way above my budget. I entered the foyer with the girlfriend and explained to the concierge that I had stayed in the hotel some years previously as a schoolchild. "Oh yes, that was when the establishment was a holiday home for deprived children."! I never knew I was a deprived child, but got back into the sports car feeling a little deflated.

A PROPER DOCTOR!

Qualification came too soon; real work was to begin. Over five years of training with a small group we had, and still remain, a close knit group. The change was brought home to me when my first job, at the West London Hospital required the on duty doctors to attend a "crash call". This is a medical emergency anywhere in the building, and all available medical personnel are expected to attend. And we all did attend, at some unearthly hour of the morning, but instead of the immature jovial students there was suddenly a circle of professionals all working as a team together. I felt both proud and humbled to be in that position.

The West London Hospital was in those days a typical busy environment, with all the usual medical specialities. Although I was working as a houseman, the most junior post, in surgery, there was always lots to do with admitting patients and dealing with drugs. The hours in those days were much longer than today, but as we were all doing the same timetables it all felt normal. I do remember not leaving the hospital for two weeks and feeling strange to be outside the building. We slept in the building and were continually on call. I had an affection for that establishment, particularly the "Special Clinic". This was the coded name for the Venereal Disease department, and I spent many an enjoyable afternoon there as a student. I did make a hasty exit one day though, when I recognised one of the patients as an old teacher from my Grammar School. I don't know which of us would have been the more embarrassed! The consultant at the time had a bad stammer, but tried always to use the colloquial language that the patients would understand. To ask the men to show him their penis, he would always ask to see their "cock". The problem was that he often had problems with the letter "C" and would stutter, "Show us your c….c….c….c…c…Old man then."

My Boss was a general surgeon who had a great interest in the stomach. He had invented a new operation which involved lots of extra, specially made equipment to measure pressure in the stomach, and which always went wrong during procedures. Instead of taking less than an hour for routine work, the operations would often take two or three hours, with his juniors becoming more and more bored. I don't think he ever knew my name, but often took me with him to the local private clinic to assist him, and always trying to speed away from me on return in his new V8 car. Our anaesthetist was trying a new drug at the time, now widely abused in the addict world, which was unusual in that the patient seemed to be conscious all the time and there was no need to aid breathing. Pain was not experienced. All went well until one operation on a lady's piles, when she suddenly started singing at the top of her voice. Not a good voice, and not conducive to calm operating, and the anaesthetist was persuaded to change the drug in future.

Six months at West London flashed by, but I was becoming a proper doctor. I had hoped to stay at the hospital for another job, in medicine, but I was pipped at the post by a colleague who has always had the talent to being at the right place at the right time. He is now a professor of Surgery! Instead I got a job at Barnet in North London, which felt almost like a trip into the countryside. I spent a very enjoyable eighteen months there, doing a year of Casualty and Orthopaedics after my General Medicine job. I lived in the hospital accommodation, initially in a bachelor flat in a large house in the grounds. There were about eight of us in the house, in all different specialities. My next door neighbour was a nice lady trainee anaesthetist, who was a very nervous sort of girl, and jumped out of her skin at the slightest interruption. At this time we did have the odd day off, and I was very keen on sea fishing at that stage. We had caught lots of dogfish on the last outing, small sharks about a metre long. I brought one home and, with fellow junior doctors, decided to surprise the young lady. Whilst she was out, we entered her room and shoved the shark into her toilet, just managing to close the lid, with the sharks head uppermost. We knew when she was to come off duty and all crammed, giggling like children, into my small room to await her return. The scream must have been heard all over Barnet, let alone the hospital!

I loved working in Casualty and Orthopaedics. Not knowing what may come in next, a drunk maybe, and stabbing maybe, and lots of traffic accidents. I don't remember being bothered too much my minor problems that should have been seen in General Practise, but we did have some very good nursing stall who soon shoved unsuitable patients in the correct direction. That has changed as well nowadays. It meant that I felt able to deal with any medical emergency, and gave me lots of confidence. Orthopaedics is great fun. Carpentry with blood. And in the wards it is the only speciality where the patients are generally well, with loads of banter, and, in those days, boozy afternoons. I remember being able to prescribe a bottle of Guinness if I thought it would help the patient, and frequently did so.

It was also the time when I really became an adult, and married. The stag night was held around London, chauffeured by my good friend and colleague, sadly now deceased. I do remember parts of it, like being left outside the curry house holding on to a lamppost whilst they all went inside, and being driven home to Casualty, where it was felt I ought to stay, resting, for a few hours! Our marriage in Lincolnshire was sunny and special, and the honeymoon to Wales in my sports car only marred by the clutch breaking in Stafford. We were directed to a local "hotel", which was cheap and a little strange, with very small rooms and a very large double bed. It was only the next day at the garage that we found out it was really a house of ill repute!

Back to work in Barnet, this time with my lovely wife, and I was aware that my stint in the Air Force was due to begin. I had already postponed the call up to do an exam. Typically, the forces refused my first request for postponement, but I have learnt the value of persistence, and on the third application they relented. Work in Casualty and Orthopaedics, and the fact that I liked messing about making things, were the reasons for deciding on Surgery as a career. The problem was the exams. In those days, anatomy had to be learned in very fine detail for the Primary examination to become a Fellow of the Royal College of Surgeons. But it was because this exam that my Air Force career had been postponed, so I had to get stuck into some serious study. The pass rate was only about 30%, and the examiners had a reputation for being aggressive and nasty. Actually I didn't believe that as, once as a student, I had acted as a model for the surface anatomy exam. This was another paid exercise which involved laying on a couch all day with little on so that the candidates could show the examiners where various bits of anatomy were situated beneath the skin. It was a boring pastime, but on in which I saw the games examiners play with people and it proved invaluable later when it was my turn to be the other side of the examination desk. After spending very many hours poring over numerous anatomy books the test was taken and passed. I now had my ticket for entering the Air Force and also entering a speciality.

THE ROYAL AIR FORCE.

I have never felt particularly patriotic, and joining the forces was purely for financial reasons. It meant slipping off a rung of the professional ladder, but on the other hand it was something different. Very different.

By this time we had all been in practise for a couple of years, were reasonably professionally competent, and has a degree of self-importance. In other words we were cocky buggers. The initial training at Henlow soon changed that. We were a diverse group of about fifteen, with several ladies included, and had to learn how to wear a uniform and march up and down with a very loud man shouting at us. He was not a nice man, either, and any personal flaw in marching technique was soon identified and ridiculed. Not expected by mature medical professionals! Actually, I reckon he had a lovely job and was inwardly laughing his head off. The training lasted a couple of weeks, and I honestly can't remember doing anything else but marching. I never, ever, did any more marching in my forces career!

RAF HOSPITAL HALTON.

In the early 70's we still had lots of Forces Hospitals all over the country, and lots of bases overseas. My surgical endeavours were mainly to avoid having to go and work on a dull military base, doing general practise and little else. One of the excitements and one of the problems in military life is the complete lack of control one has over postings, but I was lucky in being sent to Princess Alexandra's Royal Air Force Hospital in Halton, Buckinghamshire. This was then a very busy multi-disciplinary establishment which dealt with not only forces, but the local population as well. We were given a nice big house in the Officers' Quarters, and I had to wear some ribbon on my shoulder which meant I was a Flight Lieutenant. I still wasn't sure what all the ribbons meant, but the more ribbons the more important one was apparently. I hate snobbishness, and judging, by the multitude of ribbons on the shoulder, seems strange, but then I guess we had to know who the bosses were and who the servants were. This did mean that we were supposed to do lots of saluting according to rank, but I never really got the hang of that and it didn't seem to matter too much. In fact the medical branch of the service were treated always as a kind of treasured and bizarre anomaly by the normal servicemen, having automatic promotion and no real military role, a bit like the padres, and we wore a little badge to confirm we were medics.

Living in the Officers' Quarters was fun. We were mainly medics, but with some administrators as well. One Irish chap had a lovely Springer Spaniel and we were delighted to be asked to look after it for a weekend whilst they went away. Neither of us had much to do with dogs in the past, although they were to be a big part of my future amusements, but at this stage we did not have any expertise. All went well the first day, with a long and enjoyable walk for us all, but then disaster. We had thought the back garden was dog proof, but Nobby had disappeared. Panic, out with the car and a thorough search of the neighbourhood with no success. Nigh time came and went, and we were out again first thing in the morning and again came back with no dog. What could we tell the owners, who were due back later that evening? And then he appeared. Limping badly with both hind legs seemingly injured, but contented in himself. I am no vet, but could find no sign of injury in any limb, so we made a great fuss of the animal and fed him a huge meal which he devoured ravenously, and then he went into a deep sleep. We were so happy to have the animal back again, but very worried about his physical condition. The owners arrived a couple of hours later, and, feeling most guilty and negligent, we apologetically relayed the story of the escape and the wounded return. "Wounded, be buggered, the randy old sod has been on the razzle again and his back legs are just knackered after all that shagging, we should have warned you."! I had noticed the contented look on the dogs' face.

Work and sport were both equally enjoyable at Halton. After a bit of general surgery and some orthopaedics I worked in the Cancer Care Department. This unit received patients from all the services and was closely linked with the Westminster Hospital in London. We did some surgical work, but there was also lots of chemotherapy, then in its infancy, and radiotherapy, given at the Westminster. I used to feel very important having to pick up a car from the motor bay and then drive myself to London and park in a reserved area at the Hospital to attend clinical meetings. Not that I did anything important myself other than present the patients to the clever clinicians there. One day I had to make the journey by train, first class of course for an officer, and was feeling tired after a good party the night before. On the return journey I asked the guard to give me a call before my stop at Wendover, and he assured me that was no problem for a uniformed officer. Bastard. I awoke at Bristol, and had to get a train back again, and pay for it myself.

The sport was played on some wonderful pitches just up the road from the Quarters. Rugby, soccer, cricket, golf and tennis. Next to the playing fields was an old disused airfield, with a deteriorating runway. One day we were at half time during a match when we were aware of a very low flying glider approaching. We all watched as he made a very bumpy landing and came to a halt very close to our pitch. The cockpit opened and a confused looking chap stood up in his seat. "This is Dunstable aerodrome chaps isn't it" We fell about laughing, and I still don't know how he got himself and his airplane home.

Our first daughter was born at Halton, and the change in life was both profound and wonderful. A happy child, except when it was time to sleep, and the only fool proof method was to put her into my old Austin A40 and drive her round the local lanes. It was a bumpy and noisy old car bought as a stop gap, but was great for giving the wife a few minutes peace and getting her old man to do something useful. She was six weeks old when I received notification of my nine month posting to Masirah.

RAF MASIRAH.

I didn't know the place existed. It is a small island off the coast of the Oman, and contained a British airbase, some Arab inhabitants, lots of sand and rock and not much else. Despite leaving my wife and new daughter, I was excited about doing something completely different. And it was different! The base served as a staging post but also had lots of its own airplanes and helicopters. I was there as the second medical officer and surgeon, and we had our own little medical centre with a staff of about twenty medics; nurses, operation room technicians and so on. All male! The island was about sixty miles long and about four miles wide, and was a poor part of Oman, where there were no proper houses for the Arabs. They all lived in huts made mainly from corrugated iron and any scrap that was washed up onto the beaches, all closely grouped together a little way from the RAF base. It was known as the Wali camp, the Wali being the local leader, although he seemed to spend most of his time on the mainland, about ten miles away. This was a change from being in an entirely medical set up, with proper pilots, engineers, radio operators and the usual administrators. The Officers' Mess was comfortable and food excellent, with lots of the local fish, and a popular bar. It was the first time I had served under a proper Camp Commander, and he seemed a nice enough chap, but was obviously the main man, and all had to obey him. Having said that, as elsewhere in the Services, the Medical Branch were viewed a bit differently from the others, and we largely did everything we wanted and were left largely alone. Each day we did open surgeries for the enlisted men, and after that also treated the Arabs.

I loved looking after the locals. The women all wore full length black veils, with only the eyes visible through a slit above the nose, and only came into camp if there was an emergency. Wives had to be bought, usually from the mainland, and had some sort of respect according to how much they cost. Some were said to be "westernised", in that under the black clothing the latest underwear might be worn. How the local airmen knew this I have no idea. The women would only agree to be examined by "hakim" the healer, which meant me or my colleague. One particular lady, who I must say walked like a model, belonged to one of the wealthier males and was reputed to be the costliest of the wives on the island, and had come from a town on the mainland. To the excitement of my staff, she presented herself to the surgery one morning complaining of abdominal pains. I could sense the testosterone of the female deprived emotions of the chaps as she made her way into my consulting room, their eyes popping. Despite the problems with the language, we ascertained that she had some abdominal pains, and it was necessary to make an examination. She had no problem at all in removing the necessary articles of clothing, to reveal, in the lower regions, not, as expected, some classy silk knickers, but a pair of Marks and Spencer's', men's' underpants! I didn't tell the boys for fear of spoiling their illusions!

There was no dental care on the Island. We did, however, have a dentists' chair and full equipment, and a friendly RAF dentist had given me a half hour tutorial on his trade before I left Halton. I knew the principle of how to fill teeth; grind out all the mucky stuff, make an inverted cone shape and then push some filling, made by mixing mercury with something else in a lovely little rattily machine, into the hole and ram it home. How could it take Dentists five years to learn that? Each tooth has its own forceps for extraction with a special shape on the end. I had a huge diagram of a mouth and arranged the forceps around the picture, so that I knew which one to use for which tooth. Dental services also provided! I did have to pull out several teeth, and re-fix some fillings, and it was great fun. I knew that pain relief was important, so gave each patient at least double the normal dose of local anaesthetic to be sure. I did lack technique, however, and remember well tugging and tugging on a molar for very sturdy Flight Sergeant for what seemed like hours before the thing came loose. He said he was six inched taller after my extraction with all the pulling on his neck.

The Arabs, who have no teeth after about the age of twenty, also turned up when they found out that the new hakim was "welding" teeth! I did try on a couple of them, especially as the machine to make the fillings with mercury fascinated me, but I am not sure I improved them much. One chap however, was so very grateful that he insisted he wanted to give me a present and asked what I wanted. Some of the chaps had some sharks' teeth as keepsakes, so I suggested he gave me one of those. He was a local fisherman and a week later our Sergeant proudly told me I had a gift in my room. I should have realised from the sniggering, and found a huge smelly sharks' head, complete with a wonderful set of teeth, on my desk.

We did have a bit of trauma occasionally, again usually involving the Arabs. There were no real roads, only dirt tracks, and most of them rode little motor bikes. Our cleaner, Mohammed, was nearly blind, and had to feel around the furniture to do the dusting, but when he was finished he got onto his Honda and drove at full speed back home! One day his friend was brought in having a bad fracture of the forearm. We had X-ray facilities and a technician, and good films confirmed the diagnosis. It was obvious that a normal plaster of Paris would not be enough to fix the problem, but searching through the kit we found some titanium orthopaedic screws. We did not have a drill or a screwdriver however, but that was no problem with the motor bay almost next door. The team from the motor section all thought it was a great idea and wanted to come and watch the operation. I was now the senior medic, and my new colleague had been taught how to give anaesthetics, so the patient was soon asleep and the bones exposed. I have always enjoyed woodwork, and orthopaedics is just the same with a bit of blood involved. We made the holes for the screws and with the borrowed equipment joined the bits of bone together. Bugger, the screws were much too long, there was no way to shorten them, and ordinary screws offered by the engineers go rusty and become infected. Never mind, I put an extra thick plaster to protect the protruding screws, the patient eventually woke up and later we had to drive him home to prevent him from using his motor bike! It all healed up well, and the screws were removed a couple of months later with no problems.

This surgical intervention must have been talked about in the Wali village. A few days later we had another patient, one with four legs, brought in by the locals. There were herds of wild gazelle living on the island, and one had been hit by a motorbike. The poor thing was brought into the medical centre with a rear leg virtually hanging off. There was no way the leg would still be viable, I thought, but some blood was still getting through and so the intrepid team this time re-operated in front of our selected Arab audience. No way would this work I thought, but with the plaster holding the shape of the limb, the little animal could just hobble about. It was seen all around the camp over the next few weeks, but then disappeared. To our amazement, a few weeks later in reappeared with the plaster hanging off but running about normally! We managed to catch the animal, remove the plaster and it was as good as new. The story was photographed and was front page news in RAF Weekly!

Because we were the only medical care for hundreds of miles, Arabs would occasionally travel from the mainland to see us. One day a family arrived with the wife obviously very ill with a high fever, which she had had for several days. In Medical School, we had to do lots of laboratory tests which we were convinced would never be any use to us. One of them was to make a thin film of blood to look at under the microscope. We had the kit to do this and to my amazement my suspicions were immediately confirmed. The lady had a classic Malaria, and my film would have graced any textbook! She quickly got better and the family was delighted, but we refused any offer of gifts this time.

The Arabs are Moslems, and circumcision was performed on the boys at the age of eight or nine, by a visiting cleric. The problem was that he visited rarely, and rumour had it that he had gone abroad. One father was very concerned about his son not being admitted to the faith If the operation was not performed, and asked me if I would do it. I think that circumcision is male mutilation and that it cannot be justified by religion, but that is my belief and I respect that of others. But there was no way I was going to do the deed without any anaesthetic, as the cleric does, so we negotiated and he agreed that the lad would be sleeping when I operated. He did insist, though, that he be there when the deed was done. He had a few problems with wearing a mask and gown in theatre, but was very insistent about how much skin should be left intact, moving my hand a bit like our local cheese lady does when cutting off a slice! He was very pleased afterwards, his son less so.

The locals had lots of babies, but we were only troubled if they were in distress in childbirth. In Masirah the baby was delivered by the husbands' mother, usually aided by a posse of other experienced women, with no men allowed anywhere near. One evening I was summoned to the Wali camp to attend a difficult birth. It was night time, there was no electricity, and my Ambulance driver was not allowed into the corrugated iron building where the birth was taking place. With some trepidation I was led by the arm into the deep, black depths of a large shack with a glowing fire in the middle, the only source of light. The silence was total. Sitting around in the tin shack were about a dozen of the local ladies, all in their full black robes. There was nobody there with a word of English, and my Arabic was just as bad. But where was the patient? I looked around helplessly and gained no information whatever. Be bold, I thought, you are the Hakim, the healer, so look like you have some authority. I bent forward, and attempted to lift up the dress of the first female. She brushed me away. The second likewise. In the end I guess they felt that being molested by a strange white man was less agreeable than indicating who was the patient. She was in fairly good condition as far as I could make out, but obviously distressed and exhausted. Through the gloom and musty smell I could feel the babies' head, but it felt pretty well stuck. I explained as well as I could that it was not possible to deliver the child in the shack and that the only hope was to come to the medical centre. There was lots of muttering, but I remained, I thought, calm and assertive, and to my surprise they agreed. We got her into the ambulance and to the medical centre, along with the mother in law, and after quite a struggle, a fit male was born. We took them back to the camp and all was well. The next day I was a bit worried about the mother and child, so went back to the village to check on my patients. I found the house and the father, and asked how his wife and son were doing. He assured me that all was well, but no, I could not see them. No way could he be dissuaded. His mother appeared and thanked us for our efforts, but explained that we could not see the mother because she was preparing her husbands' dinner!

I liked the Arabs. Sometimes we would meet them elsewhere on the island and they were always very welcoming, sharing their meals and their horrible thick coffee. We would sit around the communal plate of food, making sure that the soles of the feet did not face anyone, an insult apparently. It was also not the done thing to have just one cup of the repulsive coffee, it had to be at least two, and beyond that an even number of cups. One day we were honoured that the local Wali was visiting from the mainland and had requested the presence of a party from the RAF for a meal. Naturally the C.O. was there, and I was amongst the two or three others. The Wali arrived with his own guards in an armoured Landrover. The guards looked very fierce and hairy, and all carried rifles. They obeyed their masters' commands immediately, but did not show much respect for us uniformed Officers. We had a large meal of Donkey meat and rice, with lots of bits and pieces in it, all cooked by the guards. The Wali seemed to eat only a big bone of meat, and we had the rice and little bits. The strange thing about the little bits was that there seemed to be lots of hair mixed in. It was short, dark, curly hair, exactly like that sprouting from the guards. We ate, but did not like the glint and now sly smiles circulating amongst the guards. Was that hair pubic?

At this stage I was also studying for the final part of the Fellowship of the Royal College of Surgeons. Most of my bookwork was done whilst sunbathing or whilst fishing from the beach. We had a Landrover for use by the medical staff, and in the afternoons the vehicle seemed to find its way to the best fishing spots, a line would be cast out, the sunbed arranged and study began. It did help a lot to think of colleagues poring over the books in less conducive parts of the world, but the fish did not help by frequently taking the bait and studies had to be interrupted to pull another monster to the shore. I was joined one day by the crew of the now defunct Vulcan bomber. They were keen to paddle into the water, and would not listen to my advice that there were lots of poisonous stonefish around. One of them suddenly gave out an almighty cry and jumped out of the oggin like a Polaris missile being launched. He had trodden, not on a stonefish, but on an electric ray. His chums soon came out of the water! I bumped into the same chap a few years later, and the incident was still very fresh in his mind, as were the crayfish we consoled him with. We bought these from the local fishermen for about ten pence per tail, and often sent them back to friends in the UK if a suitable flight was coming through. They were a big as lobsters and tasted delicious.

I missed the family, obviously, but was having a good time. The one thing I longed for was proper bitter beer, as we only had the canned lager type. This was soon remedied by a supply of beer making equipment being sent over and us setting up a small brewery in the Medical Centre. Demand soon outstripped supply and we had to pretend the stocks had been exhausted.

The C.O. left his post after a few months and was replaced by a much more laid back chap. He was happy for us to do whatever we wanted in our off duty times, behaving, of course, like the gentlemen we were. This meant we went off to play in the Dubai Sevens rugby tournament, and had a great weekend in what was then a small town. I remember having to drive miles into the desert until rugby posts appeared and we were at the ground. Years later I again played in the Sevens for RAF Cyprus, and the ground was now swallowed up by the outskirts of the huge city it now is. We also played lots of golf at Masirah, on the nine hole course in the hills behind the base. No greens, but rolled and oiled sand to putt on. The Arabs never really understood the game, and we had to be careful not to hit the ball too far as it would often be pinched as a trophy for the Wali camp! But the most memorable decision that the new C.O. made was that nude bathing would be allowed. This should not have been a big deal, as there were no women around, and most of the chaps had been on the island for some months and developed good protective tans. Good tans that is, apart from the regions under the trunks. Most had long since dispensed with the need for sunscreens, and indeed had forgotten about the damaging effects of the tropical sun, especially when gentle sea breezes are blowing. Over the next few days we lost count of the number of scorched male genitals we treated. Not a pretty sight, and guaranteed to slow down any running activity. Sport was curtailed for some time. I wanted to take some photos for the RAF news, but there were no volunteers!

The Airmen were generally in good health, and work was not pressing. It was a time to diversify surgical activity, and one day a young clerk came to see me explaining that he had a tattoo on the back of his hand which had always embarrassed him since he had drunkenly had it done as a bet. It was a big anchor with a girls' name attached, and as that relationship had finished he thought his future chances would be better if it could be removed. The skin in that area was not loose enough just to cut the thing out and sew up again, but after some thought we came to the idea of taking some skin from his upper arm and transplanting the tattoo to where it could be easily covered by a shirtsleeve. This we did, removing the female name at the same time, and the patient was very happy. I am not sure that tattoo transplant is a common operation.

My nine months away passed quickly but I was glad to be seeing the family again soon. I had been out of my comfort zone several times, met and formed good friendships with lots of guys, and done so many things not available at home. There is a wonderful comradeship when serving abroad, whether in the Services or as a civilian, that does not exist in the comfort of the UK. The overriding memory of flying back was to see the green of England after the brown of the Oman. We only appreciate our environment when has been missing for some time.

RAF HOSPITAL ELY.

Back in the UK at Halton, work continued as before, and we were then posted to the RAF Hospital at Ely. A nice part of the world, but not one that made a great impression on me. A second daughter had arrived and the family was thriving, but the noise of yelling children had to be avoided whenever possible, so I did lots of fishing in the local rivers. Eels were frequent and I love eating eels. They are very difficult to kill, however and wriggle for dear life; appropriately! I went out very early one morning, caught some eels and brought them home for breakfast. They seemed quite dead in the bag and the lovely wife, who was just emerging from her slumbers, agreed to put them in the frying pan for us. Now eels can look like they are dead when they are only stunned. As soon as they hit the hot fat it was a mass of frenzied activity, with the slimy things slithering all over the top of the cooker. The wife screamed and did not see the funny side of the event, and has not eaten eels since. After Masirah, work seemed a bit dull, but it meant I could pass my final FRCS exam and become a proper surgeon, and as a brief reward I was sent for a month to Singapore.

ANZUK HOSPITAL CHANGI SINGAPORE.

This was a brief trip for only a month to cover an ill colleague. The hospital looked after the forces of Australia and New Zealand as well at the UK, hence its' splendid name. I remember the flight to get there well, in an RAF jet liner, with the seats facing backwards (normal for forces planes, as it is reckoned to be safer in case of accidents) and having a whole row to myself all the way. The lack of attractive Air Hostesses was compensated by being able to sleep laying down. Singapore at that time was just being converted into the modern city it now is, but the street stalls were still in place, and a good hand- made suit could still be obtained for a few pounds in a couple of days. The weather was impressive, very warm and with rain thicker than I had ever seen, but the lovely food available everywhere and the lush flowers is what impressed me most. Work was easy and most days was finished by midday. The afternoons were spent by the swimming pool a couple of miles away, and, if needed, an ambulance would arrive to take me back for any emergency. A tough trip. I played soccer against the Prison Officers from Changi jail, in the grounds of that well known establishment, and have never been involved in such a violent match. But with the Aussies and Kiwis around, soccer was very much the second game after rugby.

I am really not sure why, but the Antipodeans seem to hate each other, at least on the Rugby field, with such huge intensity. Any match between the two was almost guaranteed to produce some injuries, so if there was a big match on I did not go to the pool! Most often the injuries were minor, but broken noses were frequent. Many rugby players wear their broken noses and cauliflower ears as badges of honour, but sometimes when the nose almost reaches towards the ear, surgical correction is required. My experience of relocating noses was minimal, in fact non- existent, but I was on call, and there was nobody else to do the job. I read the instruction manual, identified the correct forceps for shoving up the nose and managed to convince my anaesthetist that I was in command of the situation. Like all reductions it is necessary to pull the pieces apart and then realign them in the correct position. This was done, but my confidence in the end result was not high. It is difficult to get a pretty result from a bloody mass that looks like a beetroot dumpling. Then it dawned on me that I was only on the Island for another three weeks. I fixed a delicate Plaster of Paris splint over the nose with strict instructions to not remove it for four weeks. I have not had any medical negligence claims yet, and have later appreciated the difficulties, having my own nose broken whilst playing against the Army in Cyprus. I insisted on not having a plaster cast.

Dislocated shoulders were also common. I was quite good at those, having done many reductions when working in the casualty department in Barnet. After another match I was asked to see a typical example of the injury. It was a little different, however, in that the Aussie involved was complaining not about his obvious dislocation, but about an injury under his armpit and down the side of his chest. On examination there were deep lacerations of the skin and nasty looking bruising all around the chest wall. I had never seen anything like it before, and asked for an explanation from the patient. "Aw Doc," he drawled," it was a big match against those bloody Kiwis. I took a nasty tackle and knew the shoulder was out. Our scrum half reckoned he could put it back on the field because he had read about it in a book, and he put his foot into my armpit and pulled my wrist. Bloody hurt as well. He didn't do too well, but he is only a little fella, and so one of our second row reckoned he could do better. That bugger nearly pulled my arm off, and his boots had the nails sticking out, and tore my side. I asked him to take his boots off, but we were beating the buggers, and he said there was not time. Then he cussed me as I went off." His shoulder went back in easily, but his chest was sore for weeks.

All too soon my little holiday was over and it was back to the UK. I won't forget the steamy brilliance of Singapore, the outside food stalls and the bustling back streets, but have been saddened to find that the old hospital and grounds have long been swallowed up in the rampant urban development of the country. The tropical downpours and the verdant flowers are still as spectacular, but it feels a bit dull and sterile there now.

Returning to the Hospital at Ely was a relaxing and pleasant interlude. Lots of sport and fishing, not too much hard work, and learning lots about all sorts of surgical problems. Training in those days was very broadly based, so one day it may have been setting bones and the next day doing some basic plastic surgery. It was useful for the next positing to Salalah.

RAF SALALAH.

Having spent nine months on the island of Masirah, I did know that Salalah existed. It was regarded in the early seventies as being at the sharp end of any local conflicts, and had its own Field Surgical Team. It was a small town on the coast of mainland Oman, not far from the Yemenese border, with a strange climate which included a monsoon season to transform the countryside from hilly desert into something resembling rural Dorset. The station had been there as a staging post for many years, but had gained importance with the Dhofar Rebellion of the late sixties. Communist elements had attempted to overthrow the Sultanate of Oman and the British were instrumental in resisting these attacks and aided the Sultan. For reasons which I still don't understand, the events were not reported in the press, even though there were several army fatalities. The SAS were involved but known as the British Army Training Team, allegedly helping to train the Omani forces, but actually involved in the fighting themselves. I had visited once from Masirah, to play footy, and remember hearing the distant thunder of guns being fired. When my own team arrived, it really felt that we were entering a proper war zone, although the fighting was largely over by the time our team arrived. There were, however, still some gunshot wounds and mine injuries to deal with.

This was the first time I had actually led a team of medics. We were myself and another surgeon, an anaesthetist, several male nurses, radiologists and operating room technicians. I had not met most of the chaps before, and although they all seemed to get on well together, the four month trip was a real challenge. The camp itself was basic, although it had good bars for the Officers and Men, and as in all frontline posts the spirit was excellent. Discipline was relaxed, everyone had a smile, and making our own amusements was important. Amongst the flying staff there were several mercenary helicopter pilots, mainly Army trained. This was a hard drinking, courageous group of guys, making some good money by being paid by the Sultanate. I say courageous because one of the dangers to helicopters was the firing of SAM 7 missiles at them from the ground. Whereas the Strikemaster jets could sometimes out manoeuvre an oncoming rocket, the copters had no chance, so seeing one launched meant curtains for the crew. They tended to fly very low to avoid this problem and became very skilled.

The first day at Salalah one of the helicopter pilots asked if my team would like a ride. About eight of us were keen to go up, and as team leaded I was in the co-pilot seat and in direct communication with the driver. The guys behind had no idea what was going on, but seemed to be enjoying the ride over the local hills. It was the first time I had been in a light copter, and it all felt a bit flimsy and dangerous. "Are your chaps all pretty brave and calm?" I didn't have any idea what the pilot was talking about, and explained that I had only just met most of them myself. "OK, hold on" With that the engine was turned off, the machine fell through the air seemingly completely out of control, and I was terrified, even though I had been told what was going on. A helicopter will auto rotate, a bit like a sycamore seed, when falling, so no one was thrown out of their seats, but heaven knows what the guys in the back were thinking. After what felt like a lifetime, probably less than a minute, the engine was turned on again and we regained control. The pilot had a huge grin on his face; the chaps in the back did not. "Welcome to Salalah!" He laughed. After landing, the various piles of assorted effluents were cleaned up, the team reassured and congratulated on their fortitude. I am not sure if the episode increased confidence in the Team Leader.

Our team worked well together. Although there was the traditional Officer, Men, divide, this has never been a problem in Medical environments. We performed lots of operations, mainly on the locals, including dealing with leg amputations and gunshot wounds and even removing the odd appendix. The operating room was a prefabricated hut, with a few windows and poor lighting, and due to the heat we worked in boots and gowns over little else. Not a pretty sight. One day we had a particularly nasty road accident to deal with. The injured party needed blood, and no supplies were kept on site. Instead every serviceman knows his blood group, and a call via the camp radio for volunteers to donate was answered within minutes by dozens of airmen. We were able to take and infuse several pints within hours. I remember being hugely touched by the generosity of my fellow men. We had to operate on one man who had a huge head injury. It was obvious that he had some bleeding in his brain, and often death is caused by the pressure building within the skull. The only remedy is to drill holes in the head to relieve the pressure, and this I did, trying to make sure the drill didn't go too deep! The desired effect of evacuating the blood was achieved, but we were a little concerned when we took a pause in proceedings to see a collection of

Arab faces pressed against the window, watching intently. It took our interpreter all his skills to explain the reasons for drilling holes in their friends head.

The beach was not far away, and easily reached with my own transport- the FST leader had use of a Suzuki jeep. Somehow we managed to fit about six of us in the little machine for an afternoon of leisure. We had noticed that there were usually some decent surfing waves at one beach and decided to try our skills. The problem was that we were possibly a thousand miles from the nearest surfboard! What could we use instead? The question was answered by a visit to our medical storeroom; we had several coffins, and each coffin had an almost surfboard shaped coffin lid! Our great enthusiasm was not, I'm afraid, matched by the efficiency of the equipment; the lack of an upturned front end of a coffin lid did not make for flawless surfing, but lots of laughs were had, and I shall be surprised if anyone else has used similar boards in the Oman since that time! I hope the coffins have not been needed since that time as screwing down the warped tops may have proved a little difficult.

The camp was many miles from anywhere, and close to the sea. One day I was called to the Communications Centre to answer a call from a ship which had a very sick sailor aboard. The line was crackly, the staff on the ship were all Indian, and communication was not easy. It appeared that the poor chap had some sort of abdominal problem, and had been vomiting profusely for several days. He was unable to take fluids by mouth, and the ship had no facility for giving intravenous therapy. It is quite possible to die from loss of fluid in this way, and to avert disaster other routes have to be employed. I explained as clearly as I could that a tube would have to be inserted into the gentleman's rectum and some sort liquid inserted, preferably water containing some salt and sugar. To the non- medical this may be a surprise, but it is a very efficient way of rehydration. However, with the language difficulty, and with the poor communication, little advance was made. My initial semi-medical terms gradually eroded into more crude commands, including, I think, "Stuff a tube up his bum and pour some water in". There was a pause at the other end of the line. "Sahib making jokes we think". It took some time to convince the carers of the validity of my advice, but we learnt later that the patient had indeed been treated and recovered!

The camp had the usual NAAFI bars, with plenty of alcohol available although it was then generally difficult to obtain in the Oman. Our team was always keen to make some cash wherever possible, and indeed we had done some covert operations on the locals for cash which was equally shared between us. A few miles down the coast was a British construction company. They also had a bar but had problems obtaining alcohol, and what they did obtain cost them dearly. Our camp was guarded by local soldiers with rifles, and getting in and out was not always easy. One exception was our ambulance, which, with the lights and sirens going, was let out without question. Someone saw a golden opportunity. We bought loads of booze from the NAAFI, loaded up the ambulance, tried to look professional and eager to attend an emergency and drove at speed to the construction team. Our cut price alcohol was eagerly received, and further orders made. Everyone was happy and financially advantaged. The regular "emergencies" with the flashing lights apparently hugely impressed the guards, who felt that the latest FST must be doing a good job for the locals. We certainly were, but maybe not in the way they imagined. Looking back it was another episode that may have threatened my medical integrity, but we were miles away, in the desert, and doing it for fellow Brits, so who cares?

The locals were very keen on playing soccer. We had lots of very keen matches against various teams, and the rivalry was intense. The station was invited to play a match against the Sultans' army at their fort a few miles away. We drove across the desert for what seemed like hours until we saw the fort, a middle age type building in the middle of nothing. The huge outer walls enveloped a dirt yard where the match was to be played, encouraged by what seemed like hundreds of supporters. It was hot and dusty and the smell of combat was all around. There was, I seem to remember, a referee, but he did not seem to play any part in the proceedings, which were war like and very, very aggressive. And the main factor in the match was the ball. The local soldiers had not much access to equipment, and used an old and much worn child's ball with bits of leather hanging loosely off each side. They were obviously used to this tiny object, and the bare footed technique they had developed left us gawping and soon several goals in arrears. We did have some pride, and were really trying very hard, but to go from a proper ball on a proper pitch to this debacle with a baying crowd was almost frightening. Soon after half time a miracle happened. The ball burst. Beyond repair. It was suggested by our opponents that the match be abandoned, and that the 4nil score be retained, but we countered by suggesting we carried on using our own ball. There was lots of Arab moaning and grumbling, but the game recommenced. We could now play properly, and using lots of balls in the air, we soon equalised. The crowd became restless, and any minor infringement we committed was loudly booed. Just before full time our winner was scored. Complete silence in the old Fort. A feeling of surrounding outrage. We made a hasty exit and drove back to the camp at full speed, even leaving our ball behind!

As leader of the FST I was wrongly regarded as knowledgeable chap. A new hospital had just been completed in the town, and one day I was asked to visit and make an inspection, especially of the ward for the local army soldiers. The hospital was run by a very senior, old school, English Matron, who was very much in command. All was very formal, with me in my best uniform instead of flip flops, and a squad of us looking important. As we entered the military ward, to my astonishment, one of the NCO's barked out at the top of his voice a command in the local lingo. All the patients lay to attention and looked straight at the ceiling! This was apparently the normal routine, and Matron felt it was all right and proper. Our ward round completed, we repaired to Matron's quarters for some light refreshment. And could she drink! By late afternoon the party had become quite lively and we were all feeling very merry, and even Matron began singing. I really can't recall how we got back to the camp, but we did hear that the dear lady had been unable to continue her duties the following day as she had been rather ill and lost her false teeth down the lavatory!

In those days pranks could be played without much in the way of disciplinary action. Life was to be enjoyed and as long as nobody was damaged it was all part of the fun. One day a helicopter pilot had his birthday. We had a big party and all was merry. He, in particular, was perhaps a little more than merry, and had to be carried off late in the evening and tucked up in his bed. His last words, however, was that he had to fly in the morning and for someone to wake him up. These wishes were relayed to the remaining partygoers, and a plan hatched. As requested, he was woken the next morning and made ready to fly his machine. Unknown to him, however, most of the rest of the station had come to watch, many, like me, in the control tower. He made his way, delicately, to the helicopter and sat inside ready to start his checks with the tower, with all of us listening intently. It was going well until the machine would not start properly. Suppressing their guffaws the air traffic controllers suggested he inspected his machine from the outside. Exiting gently from his seat and wandering around he must have sensed something was amiss, and gradually looked up. All the rotor arms had been removed during the night! There was much wailing of delight and cheers from the tower. Luckily the pilot saw the funny side, but I bet he is teased to this day about his birthday in Salalah.

Flying is great fun. I have flown several types of aircraft, always not knowing what I was doing, but usually with some sort of competent companion. One day I was asked if I wanted to fly up the coast in a copter with one of the mercenary pilots. I can't remember his name, but he was a lugubrious chap with a large moustache and was very relaxed about life. We took off and were soon flying above the beach, noting the many sharks in the surf. "Can you fly a helicopter Rog?" I explained that I had only been in one on one occasion, when we fell out of the sky. "It's really easy, this pedal is for going faster, this handle for going up, and this stick for changing direction. You can see what is happening on all those gauges. Now you have a go." I am not usually lacking in confidence, but it really was quite a short introductory course into how to fly a complicated machine. I was keen to try, but aware of my shortcomings. With great trepidation I took control of the airplane, and my brain was in overdrive as to which lever did what. "Ok that all looks good, carry on, I'm going to have a little doze". To my astonishment he then closed his eyes and really did fall off to sleep. Bugger, what have I let myself in for? I can't ever remember having to concentrate so intently, but seemed to be able to keep the machine in the correct direction, and even the speed was controlled. Staying level was a bit more difficult, but I soon got the hang of that as well. Confidence was rising, but the engine began to make some strange noises I had not heard before. I had not got the hang of the instruments, and did not look at them much, being more concerned about staying straight and level. The engine spluttered a bit more and I became nervous again. The only thing to do was to wake to slumbering pilot and illuminate my errors. I had to shout loudly at him, trying to sound confident still, and he lunged into a semiconscious state. "What the fuck" was his genteel and supporting response. "This bugger can't fly this high!" It appears that my flying was straight and level, but we had been ascending since he dropped off to sleep. I am not sure how high we were, but it did look a long way down, and the engine was certainly objecting. He then showed me how to control the height of the machine and all was well. But he did not go to sleep again.

Our time oversees in the Services were enlightened by the visits of various entertainment groups. These usually consisted of a well-known but over the hill big name and then various other artists with always the obligatory dancers for us to ogle at. One of the advantages of being in the Officers Mess was that the troop were also lodged there and we got to know some of them quite well. Talking to some of the girls at breakfast, one said how she loved water skiing and was that available locally. Now it just happened that one of my civilian friends had a speedboat and skis and so we headed off to the local beach, much to the chagrin of my envious colleagues. The beach was a wide open space, with no cover, but the sun was not too hot and the sea was flat and ideal for the pastime. The shapely dancer showed her skills, swaying effortlessly behind the speedboat and making it all look so easy. I had never tried water skiing before, but it looked pretty easy. Wrong! The problem for any beginner is to stand up on the skis. To begin with one is crouched in the water, and then the force of the pull means standing is possible once the bum is free from the water. The initial difficulty is getting the bum up. I failed miserably. In front of a very attractive, amused and feminine audience. After several failed attempts it was obvious that I was inept and no longer providing entertainment for the onlookers. But then came an even bigger problem. The fault of trailing one's rear end in a jet of rushing seawater is that a vast amount enters through the trunks and into the rectum. And what goes up has to come down! My initial realisation of the extra amount of fluid I was carrying was suddenly complicated by the fact that I would not be able to hang on to it for more than a few seconds. There was no cover on the beach, only a giggling audience. Which way to run? No, running would spell disaster. Instead a steady waddle to the water's edge and an explosive release of gallons of unattractively coloured sea water. Not exactly the way to impress the dancing girls, but they had some stories to tell when they got back to the UK.

My fledgling dentistry skills were again called upon in Salalah. Another of the Helicopter pilots, who was very well known in the Mess, had a recurrent painful toothache and he decided he wanted the offending tooth removed. He was well known for his legendary consumption of beer-in particular the black Carlsberg cans known locally a "Black Charlies" and was usually seen wandering in the bar with one of these in his hand. I offered to remove the molar under local anaesthetic, as I had done several times in Masirah, but he was adamant that he needed a general anaesthetic because he was scared. My hugely competent anaesthetist colleague willingly agreed to the procedure, and it was planned for the next day. Really, I am not very good with teeth, and as the patient was to be asleep I was worried I would pull the wrong one out. We managed to mark the tooth with an indelible pen before he was asleep, and we all agreed which one was the target molar. After a bit of tugging and wrenching the offending tooth came out easily, but we felt our task was not yet complete. One of the team was a plaster room expert, and he was keen to show his prowess. With our victim still in his slumbers, an elaborate plaster cast was made, which extended from his right shoulder, included his right arm and hand, and was then formed to include a Black Charlie. The can was about six inches from the patient's mouth, but after the plaster was set he could not move it any closer. His wakening was, I hope, a pleasant surprise, and he soon saw the funny side. His tooth no longer hurt him and he was close to his best friend. That entire evening in the Mess he was seen wandering around in his big plaster cast with the can still full and unavailable. Luckily he could use his left hand for his drinking, and we removed the cast the next day so that he could wipe his backside! I guess that is another episode that would have caused me to be struck off the Medical List in the UK.

Our anaesthetist was a quiet and introspective chap who spent a lot of his time by himself. He was very keen on the local animals and could often be found feeding the local birds. But he was particularly keen on the local chameleons, which could be found in the camp but more often in the bondu. At the end of the tour he had a collection of about a dozen of the little animals, and had become very fond of them. Rather than release them back into the wild he decided to take them back to the UK. This was, of course, not allowed, but he felt it a silly rule and he would ignore it. How to smuggle the little beasts back into the country? They needed warmth, and did not mind being in the dark, so the obvious answer was to secrete them about his person. This he did, with an animal in each uniform pocket, and one or two up his sleeve. The problem with chameleons is that they do not respond well to commands, and rather that lying very still, each of them started to move vigorously when entering through customs. They were not small animals, about eight inches long, and it must have been a torture to ignore them, but he managed by looking uncomfortable and taking the occasional very casual scratch. To those of the party in the know, it looked like he was continually rippling his muscles. The animals arrived at the RAF Hospital at Nocton Hall all alive, if a little chilly!

I left Salalah after three months, leaving the team behind. We had a wonderful spirit there and some useful work was done, and I was sad to leave. We had all gained in experience and had earned some extra cash as well. The worse the adversity, the better team spirit is, in my experience, and the lack of creature comforts was certainly a factor in the pleasure of the tour.

I flew back as the only passenger on a Hercules transport plane. The crew welcomed me warmly and made me an honorary flight crew member. I thought that was very nice of them, especially when they asked if I wanted to fly the plane. Having had a little play as a pilot on an Andover, I was again reasonably confident, and determined to look at the instruments this time. My instruction in flying the big transporter was more detailed than the helicopter, and when I was given control it all seemed to go well, with the proper pilot at my side giving encouragement. "I can see that you are in control now, Rog, so we are all going to the back to have a snack". With that I was alone in the bloody great plane, trying to keep it level and at the same time looking at all those confusing instruments. A cold sweat came over me, and as much as I played with the controls, nothing seemed to make much difference to the airplane. How long will it be before the crew come back in? I didn't want to shout and sound like a wimp, so just stayed there sweating end thinking about all the disasters that could ensue. Just as my panic reached a crescendo, the grinning flight crew all came back into the cockpit. "Well done, Rog, did you know that you have been on autopilot?" Bastards.

PRINCESS MARY RAF HOSPITAL CYPRUS.

After all the fun and games it was time to be a proper husband and father and behave properly. This lovely posting for eighteen months of leisure, with a modicum of work, was good family fun. We now had two young daughters, and were well provided with a nice little house in the Officer's quarters. The hospital, built on a cliff about three miles away, was modern and busy. Work started early, usually 7.30am, but was finished soon after midday, and it was fun to get there on my little Honda motorbike, travelling across the cliff paths rather than the road.

At that time the US had the "secret" U2 airplane in operation from the airbase. A great big black thing which took off every morning at exactly 6.30am in order to fly very high and spy on all things suspicious. It was hugely powerful in order to fly at very high altitudes, and made an earth trembling noise whilst taking off. Nobody bothered with an alarm clock because we were all wakened by the U2, feeling as if the house was being shaken to pieces. Then one day the plane had some technical problems and was grounded. Without exception everyone was late for work! It really was an evil looking bit of kit which used to glide into its landing every evening making almost no sound.

Because we had so much time off, most afternoons were spent at our shared little beach hut. The problem was that we were still on call, and could not be contacted easily. This was, of course, long before mobile telephones and even pagers. Luckily I played lots of rugby and got to know the local Army lads who ran the communications on the island. No problem, Rog, we will lay a telephone wire for you! I thought they were joking, but a few days later we were connected to the main switchboard by a mile long wire laid by the Pongos. (A term of affection, used by the RAF for the Army-where the Army goes, the pong goes.) All went well, and we could lay on the sand and still hear the phone in the beach hut. As time progressed, however, sailing became an afternoon pastime, and even the Army could not lay a line to our Enterprise dingy. We got over this hurdle by the generosity of our wives, who, if we were called, would bring a big coloured sun umbrella to the edge of the sea and twist it round and round.

Work was not taxing but interesting. The locals had a penchant for fishing, but local stocks were poor and new methods were needed. They began using explosives, slinging them into the water and then picking up all the stunned fish. One chap forgot to let go of his dynamite. That was the first of two arm amputations I had to perform, but he begged us not to tell anyone how he lost his arm because the method of fishing was illegal! The second was a young British soldier who had trapped his arm in a landslide. I remember well trying in vain to join up the blood vessels to save the limb, but without success. There was not usually much medical cover if there was a problem, but I liked that and wanted to try anything new. One day we had a local man with a dislocated hip from falling off his motorbike. Nobody knew how to put the thing back in place, but we had all the books, and a nice, willing anaesthetist to put him to sleep. That in itself was interesting, because he had to be laid on the floor so that I could get enough purchase on his leg to pull it hard enough to go back in. After some tugging, and with lots of loud verbal encouragement, the hip plopped back in and all was well.

Cyprus is a lovely island, and we spent a most enjoyable time there. The weather was warm in summer and cool in winter, and we spent several days skiing on the Forces resort on Troodos Mountain. This was the summer of 1976, when the scorching heatwave hit the UK, and it was strange to meet people coming to the relative coolness of the Mediterranean island. A few months into the posting I was sent on a mission to the Indian Ocean.

RAF GAN.

Gan is the southernmost island in the Maldives. It is one of the pretty atolls which adorn the shallow waters of this tropical paradise, and served as a staging post for the RAF to fly to the Far East. It was a tough trip! The island itself is only about a mile long, had its own Medical Centre, which looked after the local inhabitants as well as the Forces personnel. I was there, I think, to perform some operations which were a bit beyond the talents of the resident Medical Officer, but went there with a physician friend who was also having a bit of a "jolly". The station had lots of coconut trees, and my colleague had read that the commonest cause of death on the island is being hit on the head by a falling coconut. Accordingly he always took avoiding action which meant getting to the bar took him far longer than it took the rest of us. None of us were hit by falling coconuts! We had to do a little bit of work, but before that managed a day snorkelling in the coral reefs which surround the islands. I have never seen such magnificent colours, the fish and also the coral itself. And I was being paid to do all this!

The locals on the island were a joy; very keen to meet us and show us their shiny white homes. The babies, in particular, all looked chubby and very contented, unlike our own second born in Cyprus, who the wife had difficulty in weaning. I asked them the secret and was told that all the babies were weaned on the local bananas, and there was never any problems. Sure enough, on my return, bananas were the cure!

The Maldivians were usually very fit, but one of the medical problems on the island was Elephantiasis. This is a condition caused by a tiny worm, which enters the lymphatic system and causes blockages to tissue fluid going back into the circulation. The name is descriptive of the appearance of the limbs of the affected individual, which look like elephant legs. But in Gan it was not the legs that were mainly affected, it was the scrotum. I had seen pictures of several of the inhabitants with scrotums so large that they had to be pushed in front of them in a wheelbarrow! The penis had been absorbed into the mass of swollen tissue and had not been seen for years. One of my tasks whilst in the island was to remove the oedematous material and try to liberate the male organ! Because the patients were generally very fit, anaesthetics were no problem, and soon my first afflicted gentleman was asleep on the operating table. We had checked his scrotum before the operation and found that it weighed over 35lbs! The procedure is not often performed, and indeed I had no previous experience nor any books to give advice, but after hacking away merrily for some minutes, I manage to retrieve a lost looking penis. It was liberated by excising most of the skin and swollen tissue and reconstituting a fairly normal looking ballbag. The part removed was taken away and to this day I have no idea what happened to it! After recovering from the anaesthetic the patient was delighted, and looked fondly and repeatedly at his old friend between his legs. Walking without 35lbs of ballast proved a little difficult at first, but after a couple of days he was almost running about with joy. Sadly we had not enough time to perform any more operations on his fellow sufferers, but did remove half a foot from an old man being consumed by an ascending cancer of his toes. I wanted to make another trip but the powers that be did not agree, and I can only hope that the other poor chaps have been relieved of their wheelbarrows!

The tour in Cyprus passed quickly, and my only regret is that I did not do an offered parachuting course because I was studying for some more exams. There was lots of sport still to be played, and it was typical of the Forces that when we had to play the Army in the annual rugby fixture all the team were ordered to take a week off to train. We managed to beat the Pongos, but my opposing scrum half caught me flush on the nose with a crafty punch at the bottom of the scrum. Because there were no nose specialists in Cyprus, I had to fly back to the UK to have the misshapen hooter rectified. The gas man who put me to sleep explained that he reckoned the medical staff were the most difficult to deal with and gave me a double dose of everything. I woke up properly two days later, but my nose was straight again.

We finished the tour after eighteen months and came back to the UK in Lincolnshire.

RAF HOSPITAL NOCTON HALL.

The RAF had lots of bases in Lincolnshire and around. The hospital was built to care for the local Forces population and also for use by the locals. At its peak there were over 700 beds, all in rambling old wooden huts, sloping down the hillsides. The crowning glory of the place was the Hall itself, a lovely old haunted building, now alas destroyed by fire, and used as the Officers Mess. Our accommodation was in a nice detached house in the grounds. This was my last posting in the RAF, as my Short Service Commission was now almost finished. I had had some good and bad bosses in my speciality, but my last was the most memorable.

Surgeons are a funny bunch. It is imperative to have self-confidence, and there is a fine line between confidence and arrogance. But there a few surgeons who seem aloof from the rest of the medical world, not because of arrogance but because they feel they know their job and will operate in their own little world, oblivious to and ignoring all the other specialities. Such was my last master. He was known as a fast surgeon who had no time for fools and was a man of few words. We often operated in adjoining suites, and he would finish his operation and then come and inspect my efforts. Soon after my arrival, he appeared at my shoulder. "You're making a bloody mess of that aren't you" and then walked away. I was stunned, as I thought all was going well. The anaesthetist, a senior man who had seen it all before, was soon to my rescue. "Bloody hell, you must be doing all right, he usually pushes his juniors out of the way and finishes the operation himself!" We got along well really, and often used to operate together, particularly on varicose veins when they affected both legs. He had shown me his own technique which involved pulling the tissues of the groin apart with the fingers rather than using a scalpel, much quicker and safer. One day we had a leg each to operate on and I was finished before himself. I will never forget the look he gave me, but still don't know whether it was admiration or that I could not have done things properly. One of his admonishments to the Theatre Sister who handed him the instruments, when he was given the wrong tool, was to shout "Don't give what I ask for, give me what I WANT!" He was well respected, and really enjoyed his job, especially when it involved operating on the local population. It is not unkind to recall that there was in those days a lot of inbreeding in the surrounding Lincolnshire villages, and some of the cases we were presented with will not be seen nowadays. I recall very well one huge lady who had a ventral hernia. This is a bulging of the guts through a weakness in the front of the belly, and it had become enormous over the years. She did not use a wheelbarrow but it was not far off. The problem with getting all those guts back into the belly is that the diaphragm is pushed up into the chest and can interfere with breathing. We operated together, and it was very impressive when the abdominal contents were liberated from their constraints; guts all over the table, guts trying to fall onto the floor, guts everywhere. Eventually after trimming pounds of adiposity from the entrails, all was returned to its rightful site and a sound repair of the anterior abdominal wall was made. I am not sure that the lady wears a bikini, but her shape was certainly much better after our efforts and she was genuinely grateful.

After several months I had learned a lot from the Group Captain and was pleased to have gained his confidence. I realised this had happened one night when we needed to perform an emergency removal of a bleeding stomach. I called the Boss, expecting him to be in the operating theatre within minutes, as gastrectomy in these conditions is difficult and dangerous. "Well, you had better get on with it hadn't you." A curt reply but one which meant I had arrived as a surgeon. All went well.

Having extended my Commission for six months it was now time to think about my future career. I enjoyed surgery, but it meant being in a hospital for the rest of my life. I had done some more exams, and was now a Member of the Royal College of Physicians as well. Cancer surgery was something I was attracted to, and I had the qualifications, but it meant going back to London and that was not appealing with two young daughters in tow. Staying in the RAF was a possibility, but the uncertainty of postings and the contracting of the Forces in general made this option unlikely. Over the weeks I looked in our trade paper, the British Medical Journal, for jobs. And there it was, "FRCS required for pleasant Wessex practise."

I had heard of Essex and even Sussex, but my geography was not good, and I had no idea where Wessex was. After consulting the books (no computers in those days!), I found it was in an historical area in South West England, and comprised bits of Dorset, Somerset and Wiltshire. The job was in a town called Blandford Forum, in Dorset, and involved General Practice as well as operating in the local Blandford Community Hospital. I applied, got the job, and life changed completely.

DORSET - A CHANGE OF LIFE.

I am a boy from inner London, but have always loved the countryside. As a student I had spent a very enjoyable summer working as a bread delivery boy in Bournemouth, so had been to Dorset before. Memories of the area had faded, however, and Blandford is in North Dorset, which I didn't know at all. I was to start work as the new fifth partner in a well-established practise. My partners were all of the previous generation and viewed with interest this young newcomer. Incidentally, at the last count the same practise has thirteen doctors! I had not done any formal general practice, and compulsory training in the art was not yet required, just as well as there was no way I would have done three years further as an apprentice. It was very relaxed and enjoyable, and I operated once a week at the local hospital, at first with my surgical predecessor. He was an ex-colonial who had spent many years operating in Africa, and was also a woodworking expert. On visiting his house for dinner, I admired his dining table. The table top was unremarkable, but instead of legs, there were carved figures of Atlas holding the surface up above him. I say Atlas, but it was a little less muscular and athletic than we imagine the mythical figure, and on enquiring it was in fact a model of my partner! He had apparently posed in front of a mirror, had a huge block of wood before him, and proceeded to copy himself with a hammer and chisel. There was apparently lots of spare time in Africa.

North Dorset is very pretty. There are no motorways in the county, even today, and apart from the summer influx of visitors, it is relatively unknown. My partners found us a little bungalow to rent in a nearby village, in an area of Outstanding Natural Beauty at the foot of an Iron Age fort called Hambledon Hill. We loved the village. My two daughters were fast approaching school age and there was a lovely little school available. The village had its own Surgery, run by a very experienced GP who had been there for thirty years. He had a lovely house at the top of the village, stuffed full of wonderful furniture and paintings. It appeared that when he began working there the National Health Service did not exist, and instead of asking for his fees, he often wavered his demands in exchange for a pretty picture or chair! His surgery was run from one end of his house, and he worked entirely alone, without any secretarial help, and even did his own dispensing. There were no appointments, and messages for the doctor were left in a little green box behind the house. He was a widower in his seventies and looked after by an assortment of village ladies who did his cleaning and cooking. His only problem was an increasing tremor, which made giving injections a procedure of chance, but his patients loved him. Not soon after our arrival he decided to retire.

Our own practise in the town had no connection with that in Child Okeford, but, after some political manoeuvres, we managed to incorporate the two together, and I was the obvious candidate to take over the village care. The only problems were that we had nowhere to practice, and I needed a proper home. The Doctors' house, as it was known, had eleven bedrooms and a few acres of land, and although it was to come on the market, there was no way we could afford it. One day our two girls were playing outside the bungalow and decided to wander off. We found them playing with a new pal a few doors away. His parents were at home and we introduced ourselves, and soon after had dinner together. They had been looking for a house as well, and as an aside mentioned how much they would love to buy the Doctors' house, but it was much too expensive for them. The wine had been flowing very freely, we were all happy, and I drunkenly suggested that we buy the property between us make it into two houses. The subject was changed and we had a good evening. The next day my neighbour appeared, with a sore head, and asked if we were really serious about the purchase. We weren't, because we had not thought about it, but on reflection it could well be the answer for both families. We bought the house together, after the owner put off the provisional buyers who wanted to make it into a Nursing Home. The property had been owned by a village doctor for at least 120 years, and he did not want things to change. Lovely man. I was asked to attend the old Doctors' leaving party in the local Hall, which was attended by almost everyone in the thousand person village. A local dignitary gave a speech and mentioned that they had had the privilege of having the same medical care for thirty years. I could not believe anyone could work that long in one place, and it was only thirty years later that I found it was indeed possible when I attended my own leaving party in the same Village Hall.

The only problem was that the house was a bit of a wreck. We soon decided on the dividing arrangements; we had the extra bedroom and they had the newer, classier end of the building. Thus began our renovation efforts. I have always enjoyed working manually, and did not think for a moment about the enormity of the task. To virtually rebuild an eleven bedroomed house into two self-contained units is not done overnight. I took a month off work, and my pal took three weeks leave from his job in the Special Boats Service in the Marines. And it was bloody freezing that January, the only place in the house which was reasonably warm was the large cellar, where we would eat our sandwich lunch. The house had no heating, and the frost even chipped off bits of chalk from the exposed wall. This is, of course, just the sort of adversity which the Marines thrive upon, and he was soon launching his sledgehammer with gusto in all directions. He also recounted that he needed to get fit for a forthcoming exercise in Norway, so the first day he put a brick in a backpack and ran up the local steep hill behind the house. The next day he put in two bricks and ran up twice. After the three weeks he was fit, but the backpack was falling to pieces, and the building was uninhabitable. We soon came to the conclusion that neither of us knew what we were doing, so we employed a local single handed builder to provide some guidance. Progress was then rapid, and after a couple of months we both moved into our separate houses, albeit with lots of work still to do.

The Surgery, situated in the old house, had been consumed by our building works, and there was no initial alternative. But small villages usually have ways to deal with vital issues, and it soon became apparent that the old village School House was empty. A new school was being built, and the old headmasters' house had been left empty although the adjacent school was still in use. We moved in. The kitchen became the dispensary, the lounge the consulting room and the corridor the waiting area. Hardly ideal, and the noise insulation and therefore patient confidentiality were not perfect, but everybody knew each other's' business anyway! Surgeries were very busy, but I learned later that most of the patients had only really come to see the new Doctor, as a change only happens once every thirty years!

THE EARLY DAYS.

All this General Practice was new to me. It was true that I had seen lots of servicemen and the families of the locals when overseas, but had never done any family medicine as such. This was before the days of specific training for the speciality and I was really on my own. In addition to my main, now singlehanded, base in the village, there were another couple of weekly surgeries in adjacent villages. These were held in residents' houses, usually in the front room, with patients waiting in the hall or outside the house. My favourite branch surgery, in the village of Okeford Fitzpaine, was a few miles away and held in a very pretty thatched cottage opposite the village pub. The road outside was on a bit of a slope, and I paid one of my early visits there in my Kit C2ar which I had assembled a few months beforehand. The new boxer dog loved the car, and always came with me on visits. He was very good and protective of the vehicle, but to start with had to be taught to stay in the passenger seat whilst I did my business in the house. There were a few patients waiting for me, and before I entered the house I shouted "stay, stay" at the dog, who then crouched down into the car, out of sight. "Stay, stay," I repeated, and went inside. The first patient came in, and in a lovely thick Dorset accent, told me brusquely, "In these parts, Doc, we just put the 'andbrake orn"

Another branch surgery was in the pretty village of Iwerne Minster. This was less well attended, and indeed we stopped the facility after a couple of years. I seemed to spend most of my time there drinking tea with the house owner, and as the visit was only once a fortnight I think people just forgot we were there. Not so for one old chap from the farm. He arrived still wearing his leather gaiters and had the thickest Dorset accent I had heard. I was convinced that he had difficulty with my London brogue as well, as we made very slow progress in communication. In those early days I was very keen and intent on doing a thorough job. It is important to take a full history and enquire about general health before launching into the specific problems. I wanted to get to know this charming old horseman, and began by asking about his general health. "Eh, whaddyasay" was the reply. I raised my voice and asked about his appetite and the working of his bowels. "Whaddysay, my lover?" It is common in Dorset to call somebody, male or female, "my lover", but I have to admit it took both myself, and particularly my wife, some time to get used to it. I persisted in my enquiries, and began to make some slow and laborious progress. We eventually came to his bladder. "Do you have to go to the toilet at night?" I asked. "Whaddyasay?" was the inevitable reply. "How is your waterworks?" Same answer. "Can you pee OK?" Same response, and I was becoming frustrated and a bit annoyed, and perhaps it showed. "How is your urine?" I shouted loudly, much to the amusement of the few waiting patients who I heard chuckle in the background. The old chap responded with equal frustration and volume. "That's what I am here for, I want a Urine (Hearing) aid"! I love the Dorset accent.

The temporary surgery in Child Okeford was not really suitable. Indeed, keeping dangerous drugs in an old kitchen larder may also have been illegal. We had to find another premises. As it happened, my own house had a large cow barn at the rear of the garage, on two levels, and we decided to convert it to a modern surgery. Looking back, a cow barn is not the ideal building, but it had lovely views over our land and further on to the hilltop town of Shaftsbury. By this time the patient numbers had also increased, and it became apparent that another pair of hands was needed. I sold the building to the practice, we converted the old barn, and we welcomed my first female partner. She worked half time, and, unlike me, had been properly trained and showed me the new and proper way to do things. We had two consulting rooms, one above the other, a dedicated pharmacy (a tiny room full of the drugs we dispensed) a cosy waiting room and reception area. My own room had the advantage of being on the upper level, and I was able to survey what was happening in our field. Not one road or building could be seen for miles, only the rolling Dorset countryside. It was a real pleasure to be able to leave the breakfast table and be sitting at my desk, away from the house and hard at work, within twenty seconds! Patients parked in a small area opposite the house, and frequently also in the narrow lane, sometimes blocking the traffic. In those days we did not have appointments, and all surgeries were on a first come first served basis. I still passionately believe in the open surgery system, but I am now an old fart and modern medicine seems to preclude that way of working. Anyway the surgeries were usually full, and it was a joy to hear the locals gossiping in the waiting room, and nobody waited more than half an hour to be seen. In fact often the patients seemed to be having such a good time that they seemed disappointed to be called to see the doctor! Every village has its characters, and after a few years I could tell who was in the waiting room by the level of noise and laughter wafting into my consulting room.

Michael Oliver was one of the most remarkable, and one of the founders of the Great Dorset Steam Fair-but more of that later. He was born and bred in the village, was about forty when I first new him, and he was short and very stubby and very loud. His broad Dorset accent could be heard above any conversation and his constant cussing did not detract from his overwhelming charm. And could he tell a story! That was a problem when he was waiting in the surgery as he soon had all the other patients attention and I could hear the roars of laughter from my consulting room. Nobody wanted to leave the entertainment to visit the miserable doctor! I had heard most of Michaels' stories by the time I left, but each time they were exaggerated at bit more, and each time it was impossible not to laugh. As time went on I began to be invited as an after dinner speaker at various events. It was always a pleasure, but impossible if Michael was speaking before me. He never had a script, but could talk for ages about next to nothing and still be immensely entertaining. He was a practical joker as well. My favourite story is about Hambledon Hill, the ancient Iron Age hill fort just behind the village. It is a local beauty spot and in a designated area of Outstanding Natural Beauty, and very carefully preserved. Each year in the eighties, a group of archaeologists from Edinburgh University visited and made carefully controlled excavations of the many burial sites and houses on the summit of the hill. These could be seen for miles around, and Michael began to spread the rumour that the local council had decided to build a housing estate for deprived people; you could already see the foundations! To say there was local uproar was an understatement! Mr Oliver was very pleased about that one. The other story about Hambledon Hill is of the Home Guard in the last war. It involved Michaels father and some of the other well-known local men, now very much in their dotage. Apparently a new warning rocket had been developed in case of invasion. The view from the top of the hill is wonderful, and naturally there was a lookout post on the top. On no account was the rocket to be fired unless there was a genuine emergency, but one of the chaps reckoned he could doctor the device so that no bright colours were emitted, and no one would notice if they fired one round just for fun. So the gun was pointed up in the air, the charge was ignited, and the mighty rocket took off skywards. Straight up into the midnight clouds. It was only at that moment that one of the team realised that what goes up must come down, and they had taken great pains to point the thing vertically with great precision. Apparently the fearless band of Home Guard ran so fast in every direction that nobody saw the returning missile! Michael has left us now and the world is a sadder place for it. Only very few people are blessed with a natural ability to entertain and delight their fellow men. He was one of them.

I am very much a London boy, but have always loved the countryside, perhaps because my maternal grandparents lived in rural Bedfordshire, where Granddad worked as a farm labourer and grew prize winning vegetables as his hobby. I loved to go and stay there and fish in the local river Ouse. And now, here I was in glorious rural Dorset, doing a job I loved and able to start messing about with all the rural pursuits, hunting, shooting and fishing all locally available. We had a lovely walled garden where I grew my vegetables, and our field of about three acres where we could keep some animals. I had just about got the house garden into some sort of order when one of the older villagers demanded to do an inspection and put me right on all my faults. "Let me see yer garden, Doc, and I'll give 'ee some advice my Luvver." The latter phrase is one I was to get used to, especially from older men. It is always good to have local knowledge, but the problem for me was that it was starting to rain. I don't like the rain and try to escape from it whenever I can. "I would love some advice Ted, but not in this downpour". I thought my adviser would relent, but no; "Zummer rain don't urt 'ee my Luvver, lead orn. An don't be a feard, I int gonna peck on ee". That meant that I shouldn't worry because he wasn't go to pick on me! I still can't remember what he told me, but do remember standing in the pouring rain receiving what seemed like endless advice. Gardening experts are a bit like Doctors in that they all have their own way of doing things, and only their way will work!

Old Bill was another local gardening expert. He looked after the garden of a local private girls' school, and grew all their vegetables in a huge garden at the back of the building. He was the first to involve me in what I call "Dorset reverse bargaining". On the advice of my garden inspector, I went to see Bill to buy some Brassica plants. He was not really allowed to sell anything, but one of the rewards for being the local Doc is that normal rules don't seem to apply. I asked for a dozen Brussel sprout plants, and he pulled me about twenty. I asked for some Winter Cauliflower plants and he did the same thing. At the end of the visit he had given me almost twice the number of plants I had asked for. I knew roughly the price of seedlings, and offered Bill five pounds. "Oh no Doc, that's far too much, give me a pound" Eventually, using all my salesman skills, I managed to beat the price up to three pounds. That is Dorset reverse bargaining, and it happened quite often.

The Great Dorset Steam Fair is an annual event which has now grown to become the largest of its type in Europe. It was started many years ago by a group of local enthusiasts who longed to re-live the old days when machines were small and simple and the industrial type of farming we see today did not exist. There were lots of old tractors and farm implements falling into disuse, especially the steam engines which are now so sought after. Led by Michael Oliver, one of the most magnetic characters one could ever meet, events began in a local field, but over the years enthusiasts from all over the country and then Europe joined in the Annual Celebration of Steam and the event now covers hundreds of acres in a permanent site near Blandford. It has become a major event in the area and roads are blocked for miles around. For many years our practice covered the medical needs of the event, with one doctor permanently in residence in a caravan, supported by the local Ambulance and the Red Cross volunteers. Each year the show is visited by some 200,000 people, with up to 30,000 on site at one time. Medical presence is required, especially as the local beer and homemade cider is in plentiful, and the evening events can be almost riotous. It was not uncommon to have the odd death at the fair, but that sad event was sometimes softened by the occasional birth as well! With so much heavy equipment about, including a huge fairground I was always nervous about major trauma, but apart from people being kicked by horses, or punched by a drunkard, it was always a joyous event. Many people stay for several days in the huge camping site, with rows and rows of caravans covering different fields. I was woken from a well-earned slumber in the early hours one night by a worried old chap whose wife was having severe stomach pains, and he pleaded with me to come and see her. I explained the difficulty of finding a particular caravan but he insisted that it would be easy, he would leave all the lights on and it was in the furthest field and would be the only one illuminated. He rushed off before I could fetch my kit, but I stomped off in his direction in the light drizzle, cussing my lack of sleep. On reaching the field, all I could see was rows and rows of caravans, every one in darkness (it was about 4am). Feeling a bit ratty by this time, I could at last see a faint light in one caravan, which was rocking slightly and a deep groaning noise could be heard from within. I banged on the door, which was locked. No reply. I knocked again, a bit louder. Suddenly the groaning stopped and a loud voice shouted "bugger off, whoever you are, and let a man get on with his pleasure". Wrong caravan. I never did find the patient, and gave up after some minutes traipsing around in the mud, but could not sleep worrying about the poor lady who may have had a serious illness. I reckoned the husband would be back and lead me directly to his caravan if her symptoms worsened, but he did not return. The next day I happened to see the chap wandering around the exhibits with a well looking lady. A bit more than angry, I enquired what had happened. "Oh Doc, her belly pain had gone by the time I returned so I turned the light off".

We had plans for cultivating some of the field as well as the house garden, and one of the locals suggested that what I needed was an Anzani Iron Horse, and as it happened he had one to sell! I am a sucker for old bits of machinery, and the local sales patter, so for twenty pounds I bought this great big heavy machine with lots of extra implements. The Iron Horse was produced after the last war as a single handed walk behind tractor for ploughing, grading and generally mucking about with the land, and was allegedly made from the remains of old wartime tanks. It is petrol driven by a JAP engine, makes lots of noise, and moves slowly on great big wheels. Without the engine working I could hardly move the thing, but was given a fools guide to using it and was then on my own. To get more traction in the muddy ground I changed the rubber tyres to heavy iron cleated rims. The only way of steering the beast was to disengage the drive from the motor to one wheel at a time, and then re engaging the drive when enough turn had been made. To stop meant pulling in the heavy clutch on the handlebar. I was so proud of that machine! Here I was, a Cockney sparra, in the middle of the country, in charge of a proper old country machine, not one of these little rotavators. It just so happened that some friends from London had come down for the weekend so I decided to show them my skills in ploughing up a portion of the field in order to plant potatoes. My little audience were impressed, I could tell, by my new skills, especially when the machine actually started first pull. We took off at the dictated leisurely pace to the ploughing area, and I put the machine into the soil and began the first furrow of my life. It was difficult to manage the heavy machine, but I pretended I was in full control, and indeed nearly was until the time came to change direction. I pulled the drive to one wheel out, and began the machine began to turn, slowly and powerfully. Then disaster. I could not get the drive back in again, and had no option but to hang on to the end of the handlebars whilst being pulled around in a large circle. I dare not let go of the rampant machine, but could not catch up enough to turn the motor off. I was being swung around like on a circus ride, and the mirth my inability conveyed was rampant. No offers to help, mind you, but crippling laughter was my only reward. The machine was eventually brought under control, leaving what looked like a bomb crater underneath it and nowhere to plant potatoes. After long and painful attempts, I eventually learned how to use the Anzani, and indeed used it in the kitchen garden for several years until I started using the deep bed method for vegetables. I eventually gave it away to a well-muscled enthusiast and hope it is still in use. Eventually the potatoes were planted, and we even began to sell sacks in the surgery. Often patients would come out with a packet of skin cream and a big bag of King Edward's. I don't think that happens nowadays.

Another tool new to me then was the chainsaw. The Dutch Elm disease had left its trail all over our part of Dorset, and we had lots of potential firewood all around. I bought a McCulloch saw, read the instructions, ignored most of them, and started cutting trees down. What fun! Great big lumps of wood tumbling over and crunching on the ground, lots of noise and smells from the two stroke motor and sawdust in every conceivable orifice. We had a row of dead elms that bordered a neighbours' garden, and my new skills enabled me to fell a tree in whichever direction I wanted. I should have known better. This time the family had arrived for the weekend, and the audience was instructed to stay clear of the landing place for the tree. The standard, angled cuts were made, I stood casually back to see if I had miscalculated by a few degrees, and was dumfounded to watch a large dead elm topple completely in the wrong direction and into the neighbours' flowerbed. I will never be allowed to forget!

Work was fun. Starting a new life in a beautiful part of the world, with lovely staff and taking over what had been a village practise for well over a century was a real pleasure. I loved the patients, particularly the locals with their strong accents, although it did take me a while to get used to being called "my lover" by some of the elderly men! Our support staff were all local ladies, many of whom had been born in the area and who knew the patients much better than I did. Lots of complicated local family relationships were explained to me and hopefully prevented too many disasters, although I did put my foot in it when I admired one lady's granddaughter only to be told it was her own new baby! Our new surgery next door in the converted cow barn was a great success, but often overcrowded. We had a little dispensary for drugs which patients could collect immediately after they were prescribed. This worked well, but we were aware that the security was not what it should be, and one night it was broken into and some strong painkillers removed. Even in those days there was a problem with drugs in the area, and gangs were known to target remote surgeries, coming from the larger towns of Bournemouth and Poole. No real damage was done, but the theft was naturally reported to the local police. In those far off days it was possible to phone the local Police station and talk to someone who we all knew. "Don't worry, Rog, we will send someone round and sort it out for you". Accordingly a visit from the local crime team was made, and the situation assessed. "We have been issued with these new alarms, Rog, and we will install number 24 in the surgery, and if it is triggered we will be round in no time and catch the buggers". The alarm, looking like a big radio, and set off by a pad under the rug in the dispensary needed to be checked daily to see if all was in order; it apparently triggered an alarm in the local station. All went well until one day the device did not work when I tested it. "No problem, Rog, they sometimes go wrong, we will send you another, don't worry, we will catch the buggers". Duly number 36 was installed and all went well. One evening around midnight there was a tap on the window of our house. Luckily we were still up, and I was surprised to find four Policemen whispering between themselves. "Don't worry, Rog, but someone is in the Dispensary and we are going to nab them". The head man was a very large Irish fellow I knew well, having delivered his daughter on the operating table at Blandford Hospital, but that is another story. I gave them the key to the surgery, tried to look fierce myself, and followed into the depths of the night to the outlying building. We crept silently and made a noiseless entry into the building, the posse with drawn truncheons. No noise from the burglars, and strangely no light either. "Bugger, there's nobody there, I'll check the alarm. But this is number 36!" I calmly explained that the other one had been changed earlier in the week by Bob the Bobby. "Silly arse, he must have forgotten to change the notice board, God knows where number 24 is now!" Bob was not, apparently, the sharpest tool in the box and I dread to think what became of him. We all managed to have a good laugh about it some weeks afterwards though.

To me the freedom of working in our practise was wonderful. In the very early days there were not too many patients, and I had a lot of free time to work on the house and generally play around. Our two little girls soon made friends in the locality, and went to the village school when they became old enough. We had a big garden, initially shared with our friends in the other part of the house, and the children often played together. The only boy, now a local headmaster, was often teased by my girls, and he sometimes lost his temper. Aged about four, he had learned to cuss at them and when particularly grieved shouted "big fat poos and bums" at them. This has, to this day, become the standard phrase of displeasure in our family! His main love at that time was to watch The Adventures of Robin Hood. He attempted to explain the last episode to us all one day, and his vivid imagination had us all enthralled. The names of the clan sometimes proved a little difficult to remember however, and he went to great lengths explaining about the big fat priest who was a friend of Robins', but he could not think of his name. His frustration grew and grew until he suddenly blurted out "yes, I remember, he was called Trier Fuck"! I am not sure whether that will be recounted in morning assembly at his present school.

The fact that we only had daughters was noticed amongst the farming community. Sons were important for carrying on the farm, although in modern times this attitude would be rightly discounted. One day a well-known and very respected farmer, Ron Millard, questioned me about the possibility of having sons in the future. I replied that it was indeed a possibility, but one had no control about the sex of future offspring. "Nonsense", he replied, and went on to tell me that if he had need of a bull calf, he made sure the cows' head was pointing in the direction of where the moon would come up that evening. "It never fails, young man, and I am the father of two sons; you need to turn the head of your bed to the direction of the rising moon, you mark my words." Time went on and in due course we had two sons. I did nothing to dissuade Ron that his advice had not been taken and he always had a broad smile when he came to see me and always asked how the "boys" were getting on!

I nearly had two sons with the same name. The first born, at home, was called Tom, and I proudly registered his arrival at the local council office. Two years later, his brother was born and it was back to the same office to name him. I knew the Registrar quite well, and we had a mutual interest in racehorses, which naturally we discussed rather than the business in hand. We had a good talk about the prospects in the forthcoming Gold Cup, and in between he dotted down the necessary information. I had completely forgotten what I was there for, and his questions about the name of my son were very much secondary to the subject of horses. It was only when I got home and the wife was asking if all went well that I realised the second son had been noted as Tom as well! What a silly arse I was! Amid very strong admonishments I meekly phoned the registrar to tell him it should have been James instead of Thomas. "Too late, Rog, I am afraid, I have already sent the documents off" His background cackling gave the game away however, and he admitted that he knew my error as soon as I left the office; he knew little Tom well. The fault was rectified, we had a Tom and Jim as well as a Sarah and Clare, and the family was complete. Job done.

The girls were a great help with the two boys, and would look after their brothers, particularly at bath time. Being growing children the inevitable questions about where babies come from were asked and we had always agreed to tell things how they are. After one long and very detailed bathroom explanation, Sarah exclaimed, unbelieving, "and you have done that to Mummy FOUR TIMES!" One of my main regrets with children is that we do not write down all their funny remarks at the time, they are priceless, but all too often forgotten.

Because I was not too busy early in the practise, I was able to work as a locum Consultant Surgeon in the local Hospital at Dorchester and Weymouth. I had gained the necessary qualifications in the RAF, and locums (temporary posts, usually to cover for illness or holidays) were difficult to fill. It would give me a chance to get to know our local Major Hospital and the staff, and also to do some proper surgery, which I was missing somewhat. I am very glad not to have been attached to a hospital full time for a career, but the challenge and satisfaction of surgery is a great experience. In those days the Consultant was someone who was very much respected and revered in the hospital hierarchy. In front of the hospital there was always a parking space for the Consultant Surgeon, and it was very well protected by the hospital staff. I drew up into the spot at Weymouth, feeling rather proud of myself, a young 30 year old in such a grand position. In no time an angry Porter was at my side asking whether or not I could read signs. I had some problems convincing him that I was, indeed, the Consultant Surgeon, but he did let me park, and was very polite in the following few weeks I was there. One night I was on call in Weymouth Hospital. It was in mid-winter, and Dorset was in the midst of a snowstorm. The problem at that time was that surgical care was shared between both Weymouth and Dorchester hospitals, and an emergency needing my attention was at the latter hospital. Between the two was a road that was easily blocked, and the snowstorm meant that we could not get there by car. The trains were still running however, and the duty anaesthetist and myself decided we would travel by that route. We had no winter clothing of note, but borrowed surgical boots from the operating theatre and made our way on foot to the local station. When we arrived at Dorchester, near midnight, the snow had become quite thick, and we had to trudge the mile or so to the hospital with fresh snow entering our white surgical boots. We both needed thawing out on arrival, but were soon fit enough to operate on a young lady with a nasty appendix. I could not manage to get back to Weymouth for several days, and indeed the Hospital was closed for all but emergency care because of the deep snow all around. We had to make our way to the local pub from the old Dorset County Hospital because all outpatient and non-emergency work had been cancelled. I recall with great pleasure sitting in the pub and watching people skiing up and down the Dorchester High Street, and feeling slightly embarrassed when the local press and television news produced a report about the fearless surgical team who travelled in a blizzard to save a young girls' life!

The life of a Consultant Surgeon in those days, was, as I say, very different. One day of the week it was my duty to travel to the old Bridport Hospital to perform a few operations. Bridport hospital has been rebuilt since those days, but it was a typical "Cottage Hospital" looking more like a friendly Hotel. I set off on the pretty journey along the cliffs to be met outside the building by the Matron, who greeted me like a long lost friend. There was no question of operating until tea and cakes had been taken in her office! How times have changed. A Consultant friend of mine tells me that he has to pay hug amounts to park in his own hospital nowadays.

The snow returned after my return to Child Okeford. The village was effectively cut off for a few days, and the two dairy farmers had to milk the cows and throw all the produce away. Eventually the roads became passable for four wheel drive vehicles. A lovely retired farmer patient, Jack Bussell, insisted that I borrow his Range Rover for a few days to enable me to reach my outlying patients. I like cars, but had never been able to afford a vehicle like that and jumped at his offer. What fun! I wanted to see if I could make it skid in the snow. I could, and only narrowly missed turning the thing over; better be a bit more cautious. A call came to visit a patient on Bulbarrow Hill, a few miles away and in the depths of snow. I knew it was not really an emergency, but decided to see if I could get there anyway. The hill is very steep, and even with the Range Rover it would have been very difficult, but as luck would have it the snow plough had cleared a way just before me. Peter the patient was very pleased and surprised to see me at the door, but we dealt with his problem and all was well. It was not until the local evening news that we heard about the intrepid local Doctor who risked life and limb to reach a seriously ill patient on a steep hillside that I felt guilty about only going there to test Jack's Range Rover! Where do these news stories come from?

It was shortly after that incident that I bought a new car myself, a bright red Renault with a turbocharger. I was very proud of it, and mentioned it to anybody I could. One evening I was seeing a new rather nice lady and she asked if the new bright red car outside was mine. I affirmed casually, and asked why she was interested. "Oh, because I have just bought a new red car myself" Without being too sexist, ladies in general do not seem to have much interest in cars, and I imagined her in a little runabout that her husband had bought her to do the shopping. She had to go and see the practice nurse, and I nipped outside to see if my suspicions were correct. Directly parked alongside my little red Renault was a huge imposing brand new red Rolls Royce! I did not boast about my new car again.

HOME VISITS.

One of the pleasures of my job was that every day I had to get in the car, drive though very pretty countryside, and visit patient in their homes. I can say pleasant now, because reflection after time softens emotions. Sometimes, when pressed for time, having to do several visits many miles apart could be a bit of a drag, and it was a joke of my partners that "Prior has patients all over Dorset". That wasn't quite true, but certainly some visits were in the depths of the local lanes, and when colleagues had to do visits to my patients they were not impressed with the distances they had to travel. It is easy to visit ones' own patients, but at weekend and holidays, covering for colleagues, journeys become more difficult.

I was on duty one wintry Sunday evening when I had a call from a gentleman with a very strong Irish accent. His wife had very severe stomach pains, and could I visit urgently. They lived in a housing estate in a village some miles away which I did not know well. It was dusk, and visibility was not good. Finding house numbers in the dark is always difficult, so I always ask how I will know which is the correct address. "No problem, Doc, there is a blue ladder outside the house". Sometimes my brain is not really in gear, and despite thinking it a bit strange to leave a ladder outside in the mid-winter, I made my way to Winterbourne Whitechuch. The housing estate in the village is easily found, but the roads somewhat confusing, and I had another call to do after this one. After circulating several times, becoming more and more frustrated, I could not see the bloody ladder. Eventually a window opened from an upstairs room and a chap began waving at me. I stopped the car." Are you the Doctor?" a broad Irish brogue shouted. "The wife is in here". Somewhat angry at the delay and my repeated tour of the estate, I regained composure and dealt with the lady, arranging for her to be admitted to the local hospital. More calm now, I quizzed the Irishman about the missing blue ladder, which had caused all my wrath. "But there it is Doc, outside as I told you". True enough, outside the house was a blue Lada car!

Getting addresses right is important. On another occasion, again at a weekend duty, and again under some pressure, I made an impressive entry, after only a cursory knock to an alleged emergency in a row of farm buildings. When a family is having a nice gentle evening in the peace and warmth of their own home, the last thing they need is a stranger bursting in and asking where the emergency is. As it happened the family were not friends with the intended couple I had come to visit, and my apologies were not well received! Here was I, the visiting angel, coming out into the wilds of the countryside, only to be treated like a burglar. Served me right on reflection.

Night calls were rare. Having one's own personal list was a great advantage because if someone rang during the night, it was usually possible to tell which patient to take an aspirin and go back to bed, or to make an emergency call. I am not sure what our patients think the doctor does at night, but do remember being called at about three in the morning by a nice lady asking me to come and see her sick husband. I agreed, but said I would have to get up out of bed and dress before coming to see him, and it may take a few minutes. "Oh Doctor, you are in bed, are you ill as well?"

I did try to maintain a professional, but relaxed approach, to visits. I carried a large, heavy bag which could have contained anything, I suppose. Apart from my name on the top, it did not look like a typical Doctors' bag, but was robust and convenient. When newly arrived in the practise, I visited a local Nursing Home for the first time. As it happened, my mood was good that day, and the Matron opened the rather grand front door and asked my business. In my opinion it was obvious that the smart young man with the heavy bag was the Doctor." I have come to mend the broken fridge", I joked, expecting to see a ripple of mirth on the stern face. "Oh good, follow me young man, and I hope you do a better job that your colleague did last time." With that she turned on her heels, and was off to the kitchen. I followed, trying to explain, but the fridge was obviously very important to her, and the speed of her walk, and possible mild deafness, made my pleading useless. It was only when we arrived at the machine and I showed her the content of my medical bag that she reluctantly admitted that I was, indeed, the Doctor. She still seemed upset that I couldn't fix the fridge though.

Nursing and Rest Homes are places we visited frequently. Most were very good, well-staffed, and happy places, and it upsets me to hear of the problems they have nowadays. One Home in our village had been taken over by a very resourceful couple who had made great improvements to the old house and had a very happy clientele of about two dozen old people, mainly single ladies, but also some elderly couples. All had their own en suite rooms, and the house was finished to a high standard, and prices for staying there reflected that. There were several very refined and delicate old ladies residing peacefully and taking their pre-dinner Sherries each day in an air of retired comfort. The village at that time had several working farms and other enterprises, including a Mink Farm. The latter attracted several protests from the Animal Liberation Front, and was eventually closed down, but not before mink escaped. I was told one day that three had managed to get out, and the owner lent me a trap, but it was only after I returned the twentieth to him that he admitted to being slightly economical with the truth. One day a particularly refined lady in the Nursing Home, rose slightly sleepily from her repose and went to her pretty little toilet room to do her natural business. On opening the toilet lid, she was more than unhappy to see the face of an escaped mink looking back at her. The scream could be heard all over the house and probably all over the village as well. Now some old ladies do have a wild imagination, and mink are not used to seeing a descending ageing perineum, so the animal disappeared back down the pipe it had come from, and the lady was gently pacified if not believed. Mink are very happy in pipes, and can swim very well, and it was not long after that a second inmate was alarmed in another room. General panic in the Rest Home, and complete reluctance to empty bowels. It was several weeks until the animals were eliminated, and order was restored, and even now, I am told, toilets are opened gingerly, and with some trepidation!

One difficulty of my job was getting to know all the patients, and how they interrelated. We lived in a very pretty part of Dorset, and the clientele was a good mix of local families and incomers like myself. The locals, with their soft Dorset accents, were a joy to treat, and always grateful for their care. I became well acquainted with a young couple in our village who were in the early days of their marriage. The young wife was a very pretty and reserved lady who seemed completely devoted to her husband and went about creating their new home with a pure rush of marital pleasure. He was in some sort of business which meant he had to spend some days away from home, but his wife coped well when he was away and busied herself with making their life comfortable. A lovely couple and an example to what married life should be, I shall call them John and Mary. One morning I had a call before breakfast to see a woman in a village a few miles away. I reckoned I could get there and back before eating myself, and rushed to the house. To my astonishment the door was opened by John, who had a couple of young children around his legs and a wheezing wife in the marital bed. What to do? He did not seem too guilty about this double life, and merely explained that his "lady" had bad asthma and could I do something. She responded very well to in injection and was soon back to normal and full of thanks. The medical emergency over, my displeasure about the social situation must have been apparent, and I gave him my most disapproving look. "Hey Doc, you don't know me do you. But you know my twin brother John in your village, my name is Jack." The twins never ceased to pull my leg each time I saw them after that.

In a village practise, there is always of lot of banter about the residents. I made it a principle to never make assumptions before meeting people myself. One farmers' wife was alleged to be "off her rocker", but managed to live a normal life and looked after her two daughters without any apparent problems. The children fell ill and a visit was requested. The mother was very well presented, very pleasant and obviously an intelligent and well-read lady. I congratulated myself inwardly for my not making false assumptions about her on the advice of others. Her husband was out on the farm, but she asked if I didn't mind having a look at Rupert as well. I knew about the two daughters, but was not aware of any other children. "Because he had heard all about you and his friends have told him what a good doctor you are" Now none of us can resist a bit of flattery like that so I agreed. The daughters were dealt with, mother was happy and so I asked her show me to Rupert. I was taken out of the back door to the yard and into little outhouse. "There he is doctor. Rupert, tell the clever doctor what is wrong with you." In front of me, on the floor, in a little bed, was a black Labrador!

I really loved driving around the pretty Dorset countryside doing my visits. The scenery changed each week with the seasons, and the views from some of the hills were magnificent. If not too pushed, I would often stop to admire the landscape. One day I saw an elderly farmer patient leaning over his gate to a pretty, sloping field on the side of Okeford Hill. He was deep in contemplation, smoking his pipe and looking as if he owned the world. "Lovely morning Bernard", I exclaimed, having stopped the car and joining him overlooking his pasture. "Are you looking for anything special?" Looking myself, I could see that the field had been mown, but there were two patches left long, and Bernard was gazing wistfully at the further of the two. "Why the long grass patches?" "Well Doc, I never mow them bits of pasture, as it's where I had my first sexual experience, many years ago now, it was wonderful, and as a tribute I leave the grass as it was." Intrigued, I enquired why there were two patches rather than the one. "That there closer one was where 'er mother sat." Now there are some strange goings on in rural Dorset, but this really was unusual. "Did she not say anything Bernard?" "Oh, the same as she always says". Strange and stranger." "And what was that Bernard?" "Baa, baa"

Being a very rural practise, any emergency often came to the GP as well as to the Ambulance service. As ever, the latter service was magnificent, but could not be in two places at one time. Some new patients had moved into a little bungalow in a neighbouring village. I had met them a couple of times; both were elderly and a little frail, but were managing well in the home of their dreams. "Doc, you must come immediately, the wife has had a most terrible accident, and she is lying unconscious on the bed. Please please come straight away" I was in the middle of a surgery, but, knowing the village was a long way from the Ambulance station, made my apologies and left. I drove as fast as I could to the village and rushed inside the open front door. A trail of blood led me to the bedroom, and a moaning bloody lady and a distraught husband. He could barely speak, but it was me who was the more perturbed when I saw a pale leg, completely detached from the body, poking out from under the bed. Trying to remain calm, I enquired how this accident happened; the trauma involved must have been enormous. "She fell over getting the post from the front door doctor. I told her she needed to put her false leg on first" I had no idea that my patient had a false leg; so much for my clinical acumen. The blood was all coming from the nose she had bumped in the fall, and after a little mild encouragement that all was not really that bad, she soon recovered.

The way patients react to emergencies has always amazed me; some are stoics, and other less so. In my experience the retired Colonials are in the former category. Margaret, ex Africa, widow of a Brigadier, and living in a very pretty thatched cottage, asked for a call. "I have come over to check the neighbours' bungalow, slipped and broken my ankle. Can you come and check me over after you have finished your work there?" After a few years, one knows which patients to rush to and which to be more relaxed about. I did not doubt Margaret's diagnosis and so went immediately. Her neighbours' bungalow was new, in immaculate condition, and adjacent to Margaret's'. "Do come in doctor, I am over here, but make sure you have wiped your feet before you do so" The order was barked out in true Colonial style, so I obeyed. "And try not to make all this mess any worse". My patient was lying on a sofa on the far side of the lounge, a trail of blood all over the pure white carpet. Her ankle had been very badly broken in her fall, the bone had come through the skin, and there was blood everywhere. The bleeding had been stopped by her application of a kitchen towel and copious pressure on the wound. "We learned how to do this sort of first aid in Africa you know. My ankle is not too bad at the moment, but look at this carpet. I can't possibly leave it looking like this and I don't think I can clean it all up with one leg out of action. You will have to do it yourself" No amount of pleading about medical emergencies being more important were effective. She refused to have any pain relief or treatment of any sort until the carpet was cleaned to her satisfaction. I was duly sent to fetch a mop and a bucket and instructed in fine detail how to clean the mess up. Cleaning is not one of my talents, and my inadequacies were duly pointed out." You have missed a bit over there, and over there. Have you never cleaned a carpet before?" After what seemed like an hour, she was satisfied, analgesia was given and the Ambulance arrived. "Make sure those people clean their shoes before they come in, there is enough mess in here already" Margaret spent many days in Hospital, no doubt advising on the running of the place, but was soon back home with spirits undiluted. A class now sadly gone.

Farmer Bill was a local character. He ran a small Council Farm locally and milked cows, all of whom he knew by the names he had given them. His farm was cold, old, and always in need of repair, and there was usually mud everywhere. He was a very large man, but not tall. He had severe diabetes which he looked after badly. A man of very few words, but lots of grunts, I liked him enormously and loved to discuss his animals, the only time when he would like to talk. He was born and bred in the area and had a very strong Dorset accent. In those days the Dorset Air Ambulance was just starting in service, but none of us had seen it yet. One pleasant afternoon I had taken the dog up Hambledon Hill for a walk. In those early days I had purchased one of the early, and illegal at that time, mobile telephones. It required a large aerial which I fixed onto our highest chimney and it meant that I now had a range of about half a mile where I could be contacted. My senior partners' wife did not believe me when one day I phoned her from the top of the hill-mobile phones were then largely unknown! Anyway a call came from the Surgery that Bill had been kicked unconscious by one of his cows and was prostrate in his field. I was several minutes away from my car, but had the brilliant idea of calling the Air Ambulance, via 999. I could tell there was great excitement from the other end as this would be one of the first outings for the helicopter to a genuine emergency. "We are on our way Doctor" I made my way down from the hill, and was impressed to see a hovering copter over Bills' farm even before I was half way down from my walk. After a few moments it took off again. Bloody brilliant, I thought, Bill is on his way to Hospital and all within a few minutes of my call from the top of a local hill. This modern technology is wonderful. On returning to the surgery I decided to go over to comfort Bills' wife and find out what had actually happened. To my surprise an Ambulance arrived at the same time as me. Apparently Bill had woken up just as the helicopter was landing and scattering his herd of beloved cows. The Air Ambulance Team jumped out and tended to their patient and explained how very lucky he was and would be in the local hospital in no time. Bill looked hazily around at the great machine, his scattered cows, and these unwelcome intruders on his land. "Bugger I, if yous thinks I getting in tha big noisy bugger you better think agin, now bugger off my farm, all of yous, I've got me coos to catch". There was no way Bill was going to get into the Helicopter, and the crew reluctantly left their patient in the field. He was a lot better when I arrived, but was eventually persuaded to go to the hospital in a "normal" ambulance, but only after his cows were all accounted for.

I loved doing home births. It was not a very common occurrence because most ladies prefer to go to hospital for delivery, and there was an increasing perception that hospital births are safer. Many would argue against that assertion, and certainly in well selected cases home delivery was both safe and satisfying. In those days we had a couple of vary experienced midwives in the area, both keen on home delivery, and we did several together. Jean Rennie and Audrey Dow had many years of experience between them, and one or the other effectively took control of the birthing whilst I generally did very little other than offer words of encouragement- to the mother that is, the midwife needed no encouragement! The atmosphere at a home birth is completely different to the hospital. There is no background activity, mum is relaxed, and we could all chat happily until birth was properly underway. It was unusual to know the sex of the child before it popped out, and husbands were more relaxed as well. I helped deliver one very beautiful local lady twice at home and on each occasion we drank Champagne and ate salmon sandwiches after the birth was complete, not like hospital at all! After one birth it was necessary to put a few stitches into a local landowners' wife after she had had an incision to help the birthing process. It was a beautiful spring morning, and the husband, who had been present at the birth in the upstairs bedroom, decided to go outside into his grounds to relax after his trauma. We all relax in differing ways, but James loved shooting. Just as I was about to put the first stitch into a naturally anxious patients' tender nether regions, a loud shotgun blast from the garden below caused both of us to jump simultaneously. He was politely asked to desist until the repair had been completed. Ladies are lovely things, and I think they are never more lovely than when giving birth.

THE SURGERY

When I took over the practise from my predecessor Willie Wilson, he had worked from what was now our home for thirty years. He was a very kind and gentle man who worked until he was 77. He himself had taken over the practise from Dr Richardson, who was still remembered by some of the more elderly residents. Before him, Drs Curme, Newbold, Montgomery and Percival had all practised from the house. Those were the days before the National Health Service, and things were done rather differently. Patients had to pay for treatment, and some of them were very poor. I am sure that my colleagues would have made allowances for those who could not pay, but sometimes payment was not financial. Legend has it that Willie was well known for not charging heavily, but would sometimes request that in lieu of payment, a family owned picture or maybe a piece of furniture be left to him. He had no children, and was quite a wealthy man, as was normal before State Educated doctors such as myself became the norm, and over his long career he acquired a wonderful collection of paintings and furniture which adorned the large 11 bedroomed house. He had originally planned to sell the building as a nursing home, and I think that negotiation to do that were quite advanced when we two couples offered to buy it between us. Being keen to continue the tradition of it being the "Doctors' House" he agreed the sale. The vast majority of his lovely collection was taken off to be auctioned at Christies' in London, but he did leave some less valuable pieces for us to use; I still have one beautiful Chippendale table. We bought the house before Willie finished his work there, and I remember fondly digging a big trench in front of the house to try and stop the damp getting in whilst patients arrived for his morning surgery. He would tell them that the young man with the shovel outside was going to be their new doctor. I am not sure how many believed him, but I did receive lots of strange looks.

Willies' surgery was one room in the end of the house, and patients came in via the rear entrance and sat and waited in what was to become our entrance hall. He had lots of pots of pills and potions in his consulting room, most covered with dust, and worked completely alone without even a secretary. Not all of the patients possessed a telephone, and many did not know how to use one. Any out of hour's messages for the doctor were to be written on a notebook left outside the house with the attached pencil, and posted in an adjacent box. All patient records were written in longhand and filed in little folders. It all sounds very archaic now, but the system had worked well for over 100 years. Satisfaction with the practise was good and there were few complaints except that Willies' tremor was getting worse with the passing years, and injections were becoming a bit of a trial. When we eventually took over the house and divided it into two, there was no room for a surgery there, so we temporarily moved into the old Schoolmasters' House while the cow barn next to us was converted into the new surgery. Cleaning out Willies' surgery was an eye opener. Potions from very very many years ago, in very pretty jars and bottles, old weighing scales (which I still have in the barn here!) and patient notes in no particular order. What exactly was in the bottles I have no idea, but remember pouring one liquid down the drain only for very pungent, smoky fumes to come up and the metal of the drain to dissolve! The splendid old oak Consulting Table and Captains' chair were to be my office furniture throughout my career in Dorset, although the latter did tend to fall apart and my welding ability in those days was not good; all my partners refused to use the chair for fear of falling out of it when they covered for my absence. Both pieces are in our office here in France now.

THE COW BARN.

Work on the outhouse was soon completed, an extension on two levels built at one end, and we had a new surgery with consulting rooms for two doctors, a waiting room and a small office and pharmacy. Waiting rooms are very boring places, unless Michael Oliver was in there, so apart from the usual out of date magazines I reckoned some entertainment for the children was needed. A small aquarium was bought and placed on a window sill, complete with a water heater and purifier. It worked quite well, but was not the attraction I had hoped for, and all came to an end when I tried to mend the water heater. For some reason I must have got the wiring wrong, as one morning we opened up the surgery to find almost boiling water, dead fish, and steam filling the room. Catastrophe! Not to be deterred we (or rather I, as the female staff were strongly in opposition!) decided to fill the old aquarium with a family of Gerbils. They are pretty little things, very active and not smelly, (the gerbils, not the staff that is) and with lots of sawdust to run around in and little wheels to play with, they were an instant hit with the children. They soon made their little nests as well. Gerbils breed very freely, and before babies are born, various activities have to be participated in. It would seem that our male Gerbil was very keen to procreate, and his activities seemed to be timed to when the surgery was full of young children and their parents. It would seem that many of the younger generation of those days had their initial education into the ways of the world by the activity of the surgery Gerbils. I had become used to parents remarking how active the little animals were, and they were certainly very popular with the kids, but one day a naughty little boy became a bit too curious and pulled their home off the shelf and onto the floor in the middle of a particularly busy surgery. The glass shattered all over the floor, the animals went in every direction, and all I heard from my room was a general shout of panic. Our lovely Secretary Christine, who was a treasure in all respects, had one failing; she was terrified of mice, and Gerbils amounted to the same thing. I left my consultation, took the few steps to the waiting room to find it almost empty of patients, the little boy very happy with himself and our secretary standing on the office desk trembling uncontrollably. Eventually a cardboard box was found, the animals recaptured, and calm restored. We gave the Gerbils away and became yet another boring waiting room.

THE FIELD.

Generally the cow barn worked well. Car parking was a problem, as although we had converted an old garden opposite, it was not big enough for the increasing number of patients and the road outside was frequently a traffic jam. The two consulting rooms were one above the other at the end of the building and had lovely views over the surrounding countryside. I had the upper storey, could see over the Blackmoor Vale and had a clear view of Shaftesbury about six or seven miles away. The view was also over our field, so I could keep an eye on the animals we kept there, and we had built a small corral at the top of the field, just below the surgery, where we could confine the animals when necessary. The only blot in the landscape was a large electricity transformer on poles outside which carried the main supply into the village. The girls were now at the local village school, the wife was on the parents' committee, and one November she asked if we could have a bonfire and fireworks in the field for all the children. It was an ideal spot, and the children would all have a good and safe view from the little corral. I was very enthusiastic, and set about building a great fire with all the wood and rubbish that came from the house and barns. It must have been about eight feet high and the same across, with a splendid Guy Fawkes on the top. I arranged a long fishing line from the surgery to the centre of the fire, doused it all with copious petrol, and made a rocket with wire rings to slide down the line to light the fire. All the children from the school arrived, very excited, and impatient for the display to begin. The headmistress gave a little speech thanking us for our efforts, and giving the go ahead for the rocket to be lit. Was I delighted? The rocket sped to its target, the petrol caught fire in a great whoosh of noise, and poor old Guy was soon enveloped in flames. There were whoops of delight from all the children, and the firework display started. It had been a very dark night, and it was only after a few minutes that I noticed my little error. The great fire had been positioned directly under the power cables to the village! Flames grew higher and higher, the cables seem to sag down to meet them, and I had a terrible fear that the village would be plunged into darkness and the transformer explode with disastrous consequences. That horrible sinking feeling which we all know became worse and worse, but there was no way I could put the fire out, and everybody was having such a good time! I am not a religious man, but I do confess to having said a few silent prayers that night. The mind worked overtime, and I could see the news reports of the stupid doctor who blew up his village and damaged scores of children with his negligent actions. Perhaps I would by struck off the Medical Register, and maybe even sent to prison. My fears eased as the flames subsided. The sagging wires sagged no more, and the sweat on my brow diminished. I had said nothing to the Headmistress, nor to my wife, and in the end I think I was the only one to notice how near we had come do disaster.

But the view over the field was very useful at lambing time. We had a small flock of Jacob sheep, smallish, black and white, and very lively. Like all things in the country, looking after sheep was new to me, but I had lots of advice, often contradictory, from my patients. One spring morning I had just got into the surgery when Christine instructed me to go immediately to the field as one of the sheep was having trouble lambing. Now as I say, my knowledge of lambing was not good, but having dealt with human birthing I reckoned it would not be too different. Usually the offspring come out by themselves without interference, and I hoped this would be the case. It wasn't. The lamb was coming out backwards, was stuck, and something had to be done. My patients were due to arrive at any moment, but I thought, perhaps, I could sort this problem out before they came. Having stripped off and washed my hands, I had a good feel about and managed to pull a live lamb out. But having read James Herriot, I knew there may be another inside, and my examination revealed that to be the case. Gently and with great inexperience, I groped inexpertly inside, and was able to retrieve and gently pull out the second lamb. The afterbirth came out soon afterwards, and the sheep took to both lambs immediately. I was proud of myself, but unaware that a half dozen of my patients had arrived and, under Christines' advice, had come to watch me from the corral. There was a spontaneous round of applause, and there was no prouder man in the land that morning!

Our field was also used to cultivate potatoes one year. It was all a big game really, because we had plenty of space for vegetables in our walled garden at the house. I got a farmer patient to come over and plough a bit of the field properly for us, as my own efforts with the Iron Horse had resulted in a useless bomb crater. We bought a couple of large sacs of seed spuds, and, with some family and some pals, planted row upon row of potatoes, probably enough for the whole village. I still can't remember why we went to such excess, but the plan was to let the pigs (much more of which later) dig up any remaining and get fat in the process. The ground was in good condition, the spuds grew beautifully and a team was assembled for the harvest later in the year. The Iron Horse did its job well this time, with the special tool for bringing the roots to the surface enabling others to follow and puts the spuds out to dry before being bagged. Planning has never been my forte; what could we do with all the spare crop? The pigs had not yet arrived, all our friends had been given a bag, and we still had many hundredweight to spare. The answer was obvious; sell them in the Surgery! This proved an instant hit, and we even had non patients coming in to buy the Doctors' lovely spuds. They soon sold out, but there was the odd complaint about wormy potatoes and them being all different sizes and shapes. We have become used to Supermarket crops now, and the real thing has lost its charm I guess. It seems a bit strange now in these days of super efficiency and over booking that we had time to sell our surplus at the same time as handing out medicines, but that was in days sadly now long gone. Life was a mixture of hard work; the patient numbers were rapidly rising and we had far more than the national average. But in general county folk seem to be much more self-sufficient than their urban fellows, and, maybe because of the welcome they were given, those with too minor complaints did not attend very often.

The land at the bottom of the field abutted on a small stream, which was spring fed from under Hambledon Hill. We have many dreams as youngsters, and one of mine was to have my own pond. In London as a small boy it was paradise to walk over Tooting Bec Common and go fishing in the lakes there. We never caught much, but I always dreamed of being able to fish in the pretty private lakes and rivers that I saw on TV. My favourite programme was "Out of Town", about the countryside and presented by Jack Hargreaves. I envied the rivers he fished in and how wonderful it would be to do the same thing. I was a little kid from London, and it never really seemed possible. Many years later, I caught my first wild brown trout, fishing in the river Piddle in Dorset with my patient, Jack Hargreaves! Life is wonderful sometimes. So the part of the field next to the stream became my dream pond. At that time home improvement grants were available from the local Council. I still don't understand how it all worked, but I applied and was granted a thousand pounds to build the lake; presumably because it would improve the environment, and a public path ran along one side of the site. A local firm was contacted, and in no time Paddy, the Irish driver, arrived with his great big digger. What a whopper it was, and only managed to get through the drive with inches to spare. Luckily the chalk soil had a layer of clay beneath and was ideal for a small lake, and over a fortnight or so a big hole was dug, and island formed in the middle, big banks formed, and a tower built in the middle to take the overflow of water back into the stream. For the inlet we led a four inch pipe many yards up the steam until it was above the lake level, and water flowed up and over the banks and filled the huge hole over about a month. Paddy had done a wonderful job, and joined us frequently for celebratory home brew beer drinking. His only concern was that our Jacob Ram, William, objected to his great multi ton machine being in his field, and rammed it with his great horns whenever it moved. The contest was unequal, but try telling that to an enraged Ram. When Paddy got out of his machine however, the contest was more equal, and the sight of an overweight, chain smoking, cussing Irishman being chased up the field by an enthusiastic ram will stay with me forever. The lake was filled with clean spring water, we added some plants and trees, and in a few weeks my dream had been fulfilled. Some small trout were bought very cheaply and thrived, and in a few months it was possible to walk down the field with a fly rod and come back with a brace of fresh trout for supper. Pure heaven! In the winter however, we did have a small problem with a leak in the overflow tower. It was possible to fix this by plugging the leak with clay from the pond, but the problem was that the hole was about four feet below the surface, easily seen from our small boat, but difficult to reach. My pal from next door, being a Marine, had a wetsuit and he offered to lend it to me to help with the repairs. It was early winter and the water was cold, but with this protection I reckoned the job would be easy; I could manage the task by myself. The suit was very easy to put on, loose in fact, but that is because my pal is twice my size. I had not worn a wet suit before, and although it flapped about a bit, the ankles and wrists fitted quite snugly and I entered the cold water with confidence. It was only when the water reached neck level that I discovered that the neck did not fit well. In fact it was a bit like water down drain hole, except that this water was freezing cold and filled up the suit from the bottom to the neck. And because it was so big for me it was like moving around in a suit of freezing liquid armour. There was no question of the task being completed; it took all my effort to turn around and stumble to the bank, where I fell over exhausted into the reeds. Cold water trickled out of the neck and I had to produce some remarkable positions to free myself from the watery torture. I had managed to do up the zip at the back of the suit, when warm and comfortable, but there was no way in my shivering state that I could reach it now! The pond is several hundred yards, downhill, from the house, and my trudging steps home seemed to take hours. No sympathy was forthcoming from the family, only fits of helpless laughter, but I was released from the blasted wet suit and took to a nice hot bath to recover. I don't think the leak was ever fixed. Our pond produced nice trout for a year or two, but became too weedy for them and eventually we put some carp in instead. I built a little house by the banks with hooks for a hammock, but I can't remember ever using it, something else always seemed more pressing. The feature is still there but sadly was left to become completely overgrown by the new owners of the property. I see on the local maps it has been called "Priors' Pond", which makes me very happy.

In London as a child we lived in an upstairs rented flat. It had a small garden at the back, just big enough to swing a cat in. No question of being able to play games or run about; we had to walk up the road to the Common to do that, but I had a very loving and happy childhood. The countryside had always fascinated me, and my maternal grandparents were from deepest Bedfordshire, where they had raised their four children and my Grandfather worked on the local farms. It was a new world to me to visit them from London, and now here we were with a field of our own! It really was a great big personal playground, from cutting down trees, ploughing the land, building a pond and letting the kids run riot with horses, cars and motorbikes. We had no buildings on the field itself, but had a couple of stables by the house. A barn was needed, to keep animal feed, equipment and to give me something to build. It is funny how some of us have to construct something to be happy. I think it all started in Bedfordshire with my Granddad, who let me use his little workshop and make wooden toys and boats. I have always loved making things and building, so a barn would be no problem. The difficulty was that we did not have much money, it all being spent on the house, so a general hunt around was started for suitable building. One great advantage of my trade is that one meets most of the local population at some time, and contacts are easy to find. At the far end of the village the old chicken farm was being demolished, and as I knew the manager quite well he agreed to sell me one of the chicken houses for next to nothing. We would have to do all the demolition ourselves, and find a way of transporting it through the village, but it was a bargain that could not be resisted. Bill Ellis, a lovely man, and one who helped us hugely over the years, and I took the old building to bits over a couple of weekends, and then John Garrett hauled it all up to the field with his old tractor and trailer. Bill and I built some foundations with concrete blocks. It was the first time I had done some proper building, and what a lovely game it is! Mixing all that sand and cement, getting the blocks level and in line, and then magic when it has all hardened the next day. My love for building and generally messing about continues to this day, and it is all only mud pies for grown up really. Anyway the walls and roof went on without problems, the windows were modified and in no time we had a huge barn, about thirty yards by ten, enough to hold a dance in! The children loved it, the horses had somewhere to hide in the rain, and later the youngest son made it into his own private den, where he and his dubious teenage mates could smoke and drink and anything else out of sight of the family. I am still not sure what else went on in the barn, but one day I was alarmed to see the local Police Helicopter hovering above! The building must be a wreck now, but Google Earth tells me it is still there. At various times the field was used for teaching the children to drive; I had bought an old car, unroadworthy but driveable, and learning how to control the machine was so much easier in a field than on the roads. It was soon used as a tow vehicle for various children to sit on improvised trailers and see how long they could remain before being unseated. The parents didn't seem to mind the danger of the games because they reckoned it was in the doctors' field and help would be available immediately. We also had a small motorbike when the boys were small, and constructed jumps in the field. Dad had to try them all first, of course, but my sons were soon much better than me. Happy days.

BLANDFORD GENERAL HOSPITAL.

When I initially came to Dorset it was in response to an advertisement for someone qualified to do surgery. The job entailed working for a day or so a week in the local cottage hospital, performing relatively minor operations such as hernia repairs, varicose veins, vasectomies and lumps and bumps. It was varied and very enjoyable work and a change from the humdrum of General Practise.

Blandford had its own Cottage Hospital. The name implies a small building, with relatively few beds, situated in a town some way from the main Hospitals. And some of them looked like cottages. Ours did when I first arrived. It had been built in, I think, 1888, by the local Lord Portman, a generous benefactor who lived in his huge house across the river Stour, and which is now Bryanston School. There were two wards of about a dozen patients each, a small casualty unit, then open all hours, and an operating theatre. It was all pretty basic, but much better than the huts I operated in whilst in the RAF. It even had a matron! Now, with modern progress, a huge extension has been built, the casualty is only for minor injuries and staffed by the nurses, and operating has been vastly reduced. There are frequent rumours of the hospital being closed, and the name has changed (why?) to Blandford Community Hospital. But enough of my whingeing, I had some great times in the Hospital, and was in there almost every day to check on my patients and to see incoming casualties. We were able to admit our own patients to the hospital and care for them there, if necessary with the help of the visiting specialists, who were always keen and helpful.

One geriatric consultant was especially keen to help. I had admitted a lovely old chap who unfortunately had had a stroke, and had difficulty moving and speaking, but who was completely mentally intact. I asked my colleague for his help, and together we saw the gentleman and discussed his problems. It was only when the foot of his bed was being raised on my colleagues' advice that the patient became very animated and was obviously trying to tell us something. Communication was difficult until the ward sister arrived and immediately began lowering the bed again. She had provided a urine bottle for the gentleman, it had been filled, but was still in the bed. He was being warmed uncontrollably from the overflowing receptacle!

Next to dying peacefully at home, I think the care in the Cottage Hospital was almost as good. The staff were all known to one another, often they were from local families, and they frequently knew their patients socially. Death is inevitable, but can often be a gentle release from this world, and with family and known staff around it is easier for everyone. One night, soon after my arrival, I was asked to visit a patient who had died. He was not my patient, but I was on duty that night and made my way to the hospital. We have all heard stories of Doctors making mistakes in certifying deaths, and it had always been a fear of mine to do the same thing. But this old chap had died peacefully and looking at him there was no doubt. I checked his pupils and the back of his eyes and death was confirmed. It was only when I came to listen to his chest that the shock occurred. A sudden "Boom" and then another shortly after. What was going on? It was only when I heard "This is the midnight news" that I realised he still had his earphones on and had been listening to the radio. Corpses don't laugh, but I bet he would have done if he had seen my face!

The Cottage Hospital was a happy place to work in. There was a real community spirit, and at Christmas, the doctors who worked there visited on Christmas Day to see the remaining patients and have a drink and mince pies with the staff. One of the doctors always dressed as Father Christmas and gave out presents to the patients and to their own children. One year it was my turn. I practised a deep "Ho Ho Ho" for several weeks beforehand and felt quite excited getting into the Father Christmas uniform. It was several sizes too big for me, but the white beard and hat felt good, and my wife was impressed that I looked like the real thing. After touring the wards, the children came and sat on my lap one by one and received their presents. My own youngest did not recognise me and sat excitedly on my lap. He looked puzzled after looking down at the ground for a couple of seconds, and then informed me "Father Christmas, my daddy has shoes exactly the same as yours". I don't think he believes in F.T. anymore!

We had a small active Casualty Department at the hospital, which was staffed by the local General Practitioners. This was usually a loose arrangement whereby any doctor who happened to be in the building was asked to see a casualty. We did lots of suturing and dealing with the more minor fractures and dislocations. Any major injury was sent to the nearest big hospital; we were about twenty miles away from Dorchester, Salisbury and Poole, each of which had a major injury unit. I liked casualty work, and had done a year in the department at Barnet General Hospital before going into the RAF. It would have been an interesting career choice, but meant being in a building all day and not having the freedom of General Practise. One day I was asked to sew the scalp wound of a young and very nervous boy. He was not one of my patients, but attended with his very sensible mother who was pleased to hear that it was now possible to glue wounds together rather than putting painful injections into the gaping wound of her six year old son. The method is very simple, a medical superglue is put into the wound and the edges held together for a few moments until they a firmly joined. I explained this with professional confidence, withholding the fact that it was going to be the first time I had done it myself. Superglue is a wonderful thing which I use a lot nowadays, but has to be respected as it can join the users' fingers together unless precautions are taken. Duly a pair of surgical gloves were put on before the glue was applied, the edges of the wound carefully approximated and held together for about a minute. The little boy had calmed down beautifully by now and we were having a nice chat together, Mother, son, the Staff Nurse, and myself. It was only at the end of the minute that I realised a small error had been made. The Surgical Gloves were attached irretrievably from the patients' head. It is difficult to remain detached and professional at moments like that, but my hands were slowly removed from the gloves, leaving a little boy with the rather unusual appearance of two flapping rubber wings on his head. I calmly explained that this was all completely normal, but may have been betrayed by the relentless giggling of Staff Nurse. She was sent away to fetch a pair of scissors. The gloves were cut off, leaving only the minimal amount of rubber surrounding the wound. Mother was told that the remaining chunks of rubber would fall off in a few days. I never saw them again, but often wonder how long the remnants remained attached.

Work in Casualty departments, when they are properly used for emergencies, is varied and fulfilling. Most of the time cases were minor, but sometimes life threatening problems presented themselves. Asthma is one of the illnesses that can be a killer in young and otherwise fit young people, and sometimes individuals have attacks which must be dealt with within minutes or the patient will die. We had at least a couple of such cases; if called to casualty for one of them it was a case of dropping everything and rushing to give a lifesaving intravenous injection. There can be nothing so dramatic as giving a dangerous injection into the vein of a dying young patient and seeing them transformed, in minutes, into normality. It happened to me several times, in casualty at Blandford, and once outside the surgery at home with the patient slumped against his lorry; he knew he was in a desperate state and knew our house. It was only pure luck that I was in at the time or he would have died from his illness. Over the years the number of times lives have been saved like that in an emergency have been few, and the emotions for me afterwards have been a complex mixture of relief and gratitude to be in a position to be able to perform them. To be trained in medicine is a privilege.

Nowadays the well trained nurses run an office hours unit at Blandford. The local Ambulance Service provides backup and I am told it all runs well. Our nurses were very competent in my day, and some of them were very enthusiastic. We were told that a young man was coming in from the local secondary school because he had sustained a very painful injury playing cricket. He had apparently been hit by a ball, but we were not sure where his injury was situated. On arrival, a very distressed young man of about sixteen came in waddling and wailing in pain and with his hand in his groin. In no time our Staff Nurse went about her professional business. Testicular damage is both painful and dangerous, and she was aware of this. Despite protests from the young man, his trousers and underpants were rapidly removed to reveal surprisingly normal looking genitalia. It was only when both had recovered their composure that he revealed that his injury was to his hand, and he only held it in his groin to try and relive his pain. She was very apologetic but was not allowed to forget the incident, and was teased endlessly. We only had to put a hand in our groin to make her blush!

Blandford Hospital Operating Theatre.

When I arrived at the Hospital, the theatre had not been changed since it was built a hundred years ago. It had yellowing tiles on the walls, no proper ventilation and an operating light that looked like a large miners' lamp. But it all worked. Dentistry, Orthopaedics, Gynaecology, Plastic and General Surgery were all performed, by local and visiting doctors. Soon after arrival it was decided to update the operating suite, largely provided for by the huge funds raised by the Hospital League of Friends. This local group of stalwarts reflected the affection the local inhabitants had for "their" hospital, and many thousands of pounds had been raised over the years. Subsequently funds have been raised for other projects such as the Hydrotherapy Pool and a huge conservatory for the patients. But the strange thing about the renovation of the Theatre was that we, the local operators and the Theatre Sister, were charged with designing the new suite! It sounds like common sense, but none of us had any experience. We sat down, did some drawings, disagreed, did some more, and eventually provided a plan which was converted by the architect into a new, efficient and effective modern operating theatre. I am not sure how many operations have been done since then, but over the years I did about ten thousand myself.

Many operations required a General Anaesthetic, and this was provided in the early days by one of my practise colleagues, and later by specialists from Dorchester Hospital. Even babies were operated on, for hernias and for circumcisions, and one colleague put them to sleep by dropping ether onto a mask, a technique which is now only know from history books. But they all went to sleep, and they all woke up afterwards, which is the aim of the game. In those days we used to keep hernia patients in the Hospital for a week before they could be discharged. When I left they departed the same day, sometimes within an hour or so. Such is progress.

Gillies' Arm.

Because I had the luck to be trained within the Services, I was happy to perform a wide variety of operations. A patient of mine had had a bad road accident many years ago which had left him with a flail arm. The nerved to the limb had been so badly damaged that it had no movement and no sensation, and just flopped about in his clothes. His eyesight had also been damaged, but he was relatively young and mobile, and was well known in the area for hitching lifts everywhere, especially when he visited his beloved Southampton Football Club. But the arm had become a burden to him; it was of no use and he wanted it removed. I had done some amputations in the Forces, and was quite happy to agree, and a date was set. At that time we had acquired our first Boxer Dog. He was called Henry Cooper, after the famous heavyweight, and he looked very fierce. In fact we had bought him very cheaply from a local breeder because his face was half white and he was much too ugly to be a show dog. We loved him dearly and he was perfect with our young family, and particularly liked to ride in my open top kit car. But he was protective of the car, and if a patient came too near when he was in it all alone his bark and growling was quite scary, especially when it was parked outside the little surgery in Okeford Fitzpaine where my patient lived. The dog would also wait patiently whilst I operated, in the car parked outside the Hospital. All went well, the arm was amputated, and after a few days of physiotherapy to get used to his new weight distribution, Gillie went home. He was a bit of a joker, was Gillie, and to all his many visitors, at home and in the hospital, he informed them that his dismembered arm had been grabbed my Henry Cooper who had jumped out of the car and run down to Blandford Market with it in his jaws. The poor dog was even more feared from that time!

Big Ears.

It is very common in country folk, who have spent many years outside in the sun, to suffer from skin cancers as they get older. I removed many hundreds of them over the years, and the vast majority cause no further problem. One of the common sites for a cancer is on the top of the ear. The skin here is tight, and grafting difficult, so the standard operation is to take a complete wedge of the ear out, like a slice of cake, and join up the edges up afterwards. The ear has a very good blood supply and heals rapidly and well, but after the operation the ear is smaller. Claud was a local farm worker who had such a cancer. He came in with his wife after she had complained about him always leaving a bloody stain on his pillow. Claud himself was indifferent to his problem but would succumb to anything to please his wife. The operation went very well, and I was pleased with myself. The edges of the wound had come together well, and he has a cosmetically very pleasing result. I saw them both together a couple of weeks after operating, and, looking proudly at the wound asked if everything was OK. Claud looked indifferent as always, but his wife was less reserved." No, it is not alright, I am not pleased at all." Thinking that there had perhaps been some residual bleeding on the pillow from the wound, I asked for the cause of her displeasure. "I have always hated Clauds' bloody great ears, and now you have given him one good one and left the other alone. Why didn't you even them up?" It is not possible to please all patients all the time.

Jim's lumps.

Another patient I didn't please all the time was a well-known local farmer and friend of mine, I will call him Jim. He had a very benign but annoying condition that resulted in multiple fatty lumps growing under his skin, all over the body. These grow, sometimes to the size of a golf ball, and become troublesome both from the cosmetic point of view and because they rub on clothing. The condition is not curable, but the lipomas are easily removed by surgery under local anaesthetic. Duly he visited us about every six months to have several of the more troublesome lesions cut out. Over the years both of us had become used to this arrangement; he took his own stitches out, and we often used to laugh about it in the local pub, where he was very well known and one of its best customers. We both had an interest in hunting and fishing at that time, and on his next attendance he jumped onto the operating table for me to cut some lumps out of his back. We were both very relaxed, me possibly much too relaxed, and I made the first incision deeply and with great confidence. A yell, heard, I am sure, all over the hospital, rang out. "You bugger, that bloody well hurts!" Overconfidence and familiarity breeds errors. I had forgotten to put the local anaesthetic in before operating! Profuse apologies were made, the local instilled, and several lumps were duly removed. All this happened in the morning list, and I was rather surprised when in the evening surgery I was asked how operating went today, and was I still economising by not using enough drugs? Apparently Jim had made his way back to the Pub for lunch after the operation, and in no time the whole of the area seemed to know my error. That is one problem in the countryside, news travels fast, even before the internet!

An unexpected bonus.

The wife of one of our local policemen worked for us in reception at the hospital, but left for a few weeks to have her first baby. She came back to visit a friend when sudden pains became overwhelming. I was in the operating theatre, before the list had started, when a colleague shouted to ask whether I fancied delivering a baby. He had examined her and things were moving fast; no time to get to the Maternity Unit 20 miles away. She was a lovely Irish lady who I knew well, and was very calm and collected, much more than I was. I had done several deliveries as a student and in the RAF, but it was not my speciality. I knew which part of the body was involved, but was a little reluctant to delve too deeply too soon. Once on the operating table it all went smoothly; the theatre sister had had a family herself, and gave soothing words at one end, and I caught the issuing infant at the other. The little operating theatre was filled with the wailing of a new born girl, apparently the first born in the hospital for very many years. The operating list was a delayed a little that morning, but after explaining the reason for the delay everyone was happy. Especially myself; there is something very special about attending childbirth, and I was very keen to extend it into my general practise. Over the years, on several occasions, I looked after the daughters of mothers I had helped deliver many years before. That is what the job is all about.

Much of the work in theatre was removing unwanted bits and pieces, warts, cancers, and general lumps and bumps. I removed a few unwanted tattoos as well. One chap I remember well wanted one removed from the back of his leg. Apparently it had been done by one of his chums when they were both more than slightly inebriated, and I had seen it in the surgery and it would be easy to remove. I had not appreciated that he was very widely adorned with professional tattoos elsewhere, and it was only when he stripped off to his underpants to get onto the table that we could all see the artistic work that had been done on his back. The whole area was covered by a hunting scene, with horses, dogs and hunters. It was a real work of art, very carefully done over very many painful hours, and we all took time to admire it. The pain involved must have been particularly severe in one area: the hunting scene involved a fox going to his hole in the ground and disappearing. The hole involved was the gentleman's' anus!

Vasectomies.

The one operation I performed more than any other was vasectomy. It is a simple procedure for the surgeon, but not always simple for the patient. To understand what it must feel like for a healthy chap to have his family jewels firstly exposed and then attacked with a scalpel by a complete stranger, competence unknown, is unsettling in the extreme. We surgeons tend to develop a matter of fact attitude to procedures, and I had to continually remind myself of the mental as well as physical trauma my patients were going through. Interestingly the operation is virtually unknown here in France, which probably says more about the French than about our stoic Englishmen. The vast majority were done under local anaesthetic (which I never forgot to put in!), although we could also offer general anaesthetic for those who really were terrified of remaining awake. The latter method was much easier to perform, and much quicker as the patient did not have to be chatted to and gentle wound infiltration with local anaesthetic was not required. My record time was 2minutes and 10 seconds, but we felt trying to improve on the record was probably not medically justified. We operated in the Surgery at Blandford as well as in the Hospital, and patients came from all over the area as we could offer a shorter waiting list and a polished service. Princess Anne made an official visit to the Hospital one year, but I do not think she really believed me when, asked what my job was, I replied that I was the North Dorset Vasectomist. She declined to question me more closely and moved on, and I have often wondered why.

The procedure is really quite simple; the tubes which come from the testes, which look like a bit of spaghetti, and carry the sperm to the outside, are tied through an incision into the ball bag (scrotum) and then replaced, usually with a stitch to the skin wound. The sperm are still produced but absorbed, and performance is the same because most of the ejaculate comes from further down the tubes and is unaffected.

I enjoyed the operation because it was obvious that most patients were nervous, and if I could put them at ease we all felt better. Some were confident, some less so, and some absolutely terrified. We always chatted about hobbies, jobs, the news and so on, and I can't think of any other situation where the truth is told so freely. I am certain I could have done some good deals with the salesmen who came in, but again professionalism precluded it. Some errors, as always, were made; often when trying to be jocular. I remember a tough looking farmer coming in and I thought he would be a stoic chap. I knew he kept pigs, and as part of his job, castrated them. When he asked what I would be doing, I replied, with a straight face, and using the farming terms, that we would "slit the purse and let the stones out". He was not amused.

After the operation the patient would get off the table and walk gingerly to the recovery room for a rest. They were asked to hold a dressing on the wound whilst walking and it was normally not a problem. One day the sister saw that a patient was not holding his dressing as requested, and called out "hold on tight otherwise it will all fall off". The patient did not appreciate that it was the dressing being referred to and envisaged rather more falling off. His grip suddenly became firm just as his colour faded from his face. Despite always trying to explain in detail what was about to happen, communication sometimes failed, not doubt due to nervousness. Another day we had a small problem with a dressing stuck to the operating gown, and it had to be removed with scissors. Again it was sister upsetting the patient "don't worry, the doctor has cut it off". Again some confusion and a hasty look under the operating gown to see is all was indeed attached that should be attached!

I am unaware of any lasting effect I have had on the local population other than having potentially reduced it by several thousand!

THE NEW SURGERY.

As time went on we outgrew the Cow Barn. The Practise list had grown from a thousand or so to well over four thousand. I had initially worked in the bigger Blandford branch of the firm, and many patients had transferred from there to Child Okeford. And Anne Thomas, my lady partner was very popular and helped swell the numbers. The orchard next door to our house came on the market. It was prime building land and a row of houses could easily have been built there, to the financial advantage of the owners, the local Wareham family. They were amongst the few remaining true villagers, who had lived there all their lives, and their ancestors before them. I knew I had arrived in the village when I could eventually understand the Warehams' thick Dorset accent. We had a few informal discussions and it was agreed the land would be sold to us to build a new Surgery. The Parish Council, which was quite a powerful influence, was behind the plan and permission for construction was easily obtained. A local firm of architects who had built several surgeries, was employed, the drawings perused by us all. It looked like a palace compared to the Cow Barn, and even had a big car parking area and a garden behind the building. My colleague John Evans and I had a lovely few days cutting the trees in the orchard with our chainsaws. They were all past their best by many years but made excellent firewood at least that is what we told ourselves, it was all another game again. After listening to patients problems all week there is nothing better than making a noise with a hot smoking machine and making lots of mess. And we lit big bonfires too; absolute heaven.

Building seems to take a long time. In fact the builders were very efficient, and as the site was on a slope tons of soil had to be moved before the foundations could be laid. The building was adjacent to our house, and one of the first things we did was to build a gate from our drive to the new site. It meant that to get to work I would now have to walk all of about fifty yards rather than the ten yards to the Cow Barn, but I reckoned the exercise would do me good. A condition of planning was that we had to replant native trees to replace the one we took out, but we were able to preserve some of the originals as well. I even planted a Horse Chestnut seedling we had grown from a conker, and it makes me feel very old to see the tree now many feet tall and producing fruit of its own. At last the building was completed, all the new kit installed and we moved to our new palace. The Opening Ceremony required a local dignitary, known to all of us, and naturally Michael Oliver was asked to officiate. He was, to my surprise, quite nervous with all the assembled professionals in front of him, but, as usual, without any notes, gave a superb address which had us all in stitches. The reception area was well stocked with leaflets of all kinds, mostly about medical conditions, but with some general reading as well. One local elderly gentleman was looking at a leaflet about Vaginal Thrush. He was not the most educated of the villagers, and looked a bit stumped by it all. He called one of the receptionists over. "This is all very interesting about this thrush stuff my dear, but have you got anything about Budgies?"

I had lost my superb view over our field, but still looked out over the lovely Blackmore Vale. Our Consulting Rooms were comfortable and relatively plush, but I am not a fan of things being too clinical and so bought a nice red sofa to have a spot to relax in. My colleagues were not in agreement with this lowering of standards, but in those days we were allowed to act as individuals and I did so. Ditto with the lawned area at the back of the building. It was about the size of a Tennis Court, was cut off from public access and doing nothing useful at all. The obvious place to keep chickens and ducks! Again I was not popular with Doctor and Management colleagues, but the other staff thought it a great idea. We had had a few fowl in the garden at home but this was much better! A new chicken house was needed, and after asking each and every patient if they knew of one, a friend at Winterbourne Stickland said she had an old house on wheels which we could have for nothing. She would be pleased to have the old thing out of her property. Bill Ellis, my trusty helper in all things, and I went to see the thing. It was certainly big enough, about fifty chickens with ease, and was still in solid condition and on big iron wheels. It had not been moved for many years, but after a bit of digging out we managed to pull the house free with the aid of my trusty four wheel drive Datsun Patrol. We did not have a trailer, but the wheels all went round as so we thought it would not be a problem to gently tow it back behind the car. This was completely illegal of course, but one advantage of being the local GP is that the local coppers are all well known to us and I am sure would have helped rather than apprehended! Using our natural intelligence, we reckoned a rope would not be ideal because we had some hills to go down and the house had no facility for stopping. A thick iron bar was attached with heavy bolts to the front axle and thence to the Datsun. We carefully advanced down the drive from the house and onto the road back to Child Okeford. All seemed well. The car was powerful enough to pull the heavy load to the top of Okeford Hill, where there is a wonderful view of the surrounding vale. We paused a moment and I felt like King of the World, a real country boy now, pulling a new home behind me for all the lucky poultry. The descent was when the problems occurred. It was a good idea to have a solid bar rather than a rope, but we had not reckoned with the house having no steering as well as no brakes. The hill is very steep and half way down we felt like we were being overtaken by something. The chicken house had a mind of its own and wanted to get to the bottom first, and had slid to the outside on the bar and was filling my far side mirror. The only thing to do was to accelerate and try to get the house behind again. At the bottom of the hill there are a couple of bends and a junction with another road before the land levels again at Okeford Fitzpaine. There was no way I could stop and slowing down had to be done on level ground. I still wonder how we managed to get round the bends and thank God that nothing was on the other road, but we made it. The iron wheels were still attached to the Hen House, but were smoking and almost red hot. After a pause to calm ourselves the journey was resumed and the house positioned at the back of the surgery. That old house housed dozens of chickens and ducks over the years, and it bought tears to my eyes when it was eventually burnt.

We bought the old Cow Barn back from the Practise, and converted it into a private house. I had negotiated an access through the new Surgery grounds and a track was laid. It meant that the property could be rented out and it would not affect our own privacy at Yew Hedge House. The conversion of the barn was relatively easy, as the plumbing and electrics were all in place, and we employed Dave Hall to do the building. Dave could do anything, and worked alone. He was a big chap, especially in the middle regions, and the only time I can remember him struggling was when he had to get under the suspended floor to get to some piping. His girth was such that entry was accomplished, but exit more difficult. The more the poor man cussed and sweated, the larger he seemed to become, and it took a rescue attempt by removing flooring to aid his escape. But a good job was done, we made a little garden, and the property was rented out for several years and then eventually sold. We called it Bovery Cottage after its bovine origins.

Our splendid new building worked very well. Except for one toilet. Builders are clever chaps usually, but had somehow failed to appreciate that water and other fluids only run downhill. The drain was on the level, and rodding out the offending pipe became an almost weekly procedure. Failure of the system was not a good advertisement for a surgery! But the other features were a pleasure. The dispensers now had a larger room for the drugs, the secretary had her own room, there was a treatment room for the nurses, and the waiting area was now much larger and comfortable. It was not the old thing though, and the genial overcrowding of the old barn was one thing I missed. At about this time the first computers came into use. Beforehand we wrote in the "Lloyd George" envelopes that were filed in countless shelves in alphabetical order. The folders had to be kept but computers were the way forward. I don't like, and have not embraced, new technology. If it can't be fixed with a hammer and screwdriver it is too complicated for me. But it was necessary to change old ways, and I was determined to learn to touch type. After many months of practise, I was competent. We all have ways of consulting, but to me it is important to look the patient in the eye, and not have a great big desk in between. My patient came in and I looked her in the eye whilst typing away professionally. She looked impressed, and I was very pleased with myself. It was only when she had left the room and I examined the notes that it was obvious that I had missed so many keys that all my typing was absolute nonsense! It took me several more years to approach efficiency. Bloody computers!

But work was not all nose to the grindstone. The chicken house had its new position and I built a shallow pond in the middle of the lawn. Both Anne and I had consulting rooms that looked over the grounds and soon they were filled with poultry of all shapes, sizes and genders. We transferred our flock from the house garden, took in any waifs and strays that patients brought in and also bought some ducks. There was no peripheral fencing, but I adapted an old electric sheep fence which worked off mains electricity and gave a good jolt to anything that wanted to escape. It was not long before one particular patient found another use for it. Bill Hands was a true country gent with only a passing belief in modern medicine. He kept some animals of his own, but never had a good electric fence. When he came to the surgery the first thing he did was to visit the poultry and grab hold of the pulsing wire. He could be seen visibly jolting with the rhythmic passing of the current, and held on, grimacing, for a minute or so. I asked him what he was doing. "Tha's much better than them pills you give me doc, fixes the joints up fine for a month or more". If it works and does not do any apparent harm then why interfere? Bill continued with his therapy on a regular basis for several years.

Chickens are good fun, and we had a selection of Bantams and regular size hens which provided loads of eggs. After supplying the staff there were still some left over and we sold them over the dispensing counter. Like the spuds, they were sought after and people often came in first thing on a Monday to buy the weekend eggs rather than for medical care. The hens began to breed, as initially we had one cockerel, and naturally we ended up with rather more males than we wanted. Chickens have individual characteristics just like we humans do, and it was not long before some of the cocks were seen to have certain traits they shared with the patients.

Accordingly they were named after the clients. Jack Hooper was a small, loud, sociable and occasionally stroppy local farmer. He later provided me with my first horse, but more of that later. Anyway, one of the Bantam cocks became Jack Hooper. Another was much larger, regal in appearance, who strode around looking important but in fact did very little. He fitted exactly the characteristics of a wealthy, tall local landowner and was called The Major after Major Roger Humphries. Yet another was probably the most attractive of all the birds, with very long and luxuriant neck feathers, an engaging personality and the life and soul of the party. We had a very glamorous patient of debateable sexuality who gave the name of Fleur to our chicken. Other names I have forgotten, but it was a real treasure to be able to sit with the staff in our coffee breaks, looking over the flock and comparing the actions of the individual birds with the human equivalents. But chickens are not the only poultry, and after a few months we acquired some ducks. Indian Runners. To those who don't know the breed they are missing hugely on entertainment. Imagine a normal duck, pulled from beak and tail at the same time so that they are elongated and that is an Indian Runner. They stand erect like penguins, and do not waddle but, as the name suggests, they run. They lay lots of eggs and form little family groups and are the most amusing animals to watch. I had to turn my consulting chair away from the window because watching the Indian Runners was often far more interesting than the patient in front of me! I found that they liked laying their eggs in old milk churns, and we put several in the run. The eggs were always laid in the far end of the churn which made retrieval difficult, but they produced chicks and the eggs, in my opinion, are much more tasty than hens' eggs. Runners can't fly so they were easy to keep in the enclosure. Not so with the Muscovy Ducks. These are much bigger animals, valued for their meat, and are altogether different. They escape with ease but are a bit like cats in that they do their own thing but know where the food comes from, and will always be around at mealtimes. For some reason they seemed to like to escape to the car park in the front of the building and waddle about as if they owned the place. Patients often had to make their way from parking the car through a melee of quacking ducks. And the main problem with Muscovy Ducks, as with geese, is that they have the amazing talent to seem to produce more excrement than the food they have eaten. Piles of duck poo at the entrance to a Doctors' surgery is not really conducive to good Health and Safety conduct, and for once Jane, our Practise Manager, was right to insist the flock was culled. In fact she needn't have worried as a few days after agreeing to rehouse them at my pond, the fox got in and killed the lot. He must have jumped the electric fence, but ran out of energy because most of the chickens and all of the Indian Runners escaped slaughter. I don't think I could work in an enclosed office with nothing to look out onto. There was always something going on. I only learnt about the mating of ducks by direct observation. No it wasn't really voyeurism, just happening to be there looking out of my window. The drake grabs the duck by the nape of the neck, thrusts her head under the water, and does his job after jumping onto her back. It became a common and frequently observed act during spring especially, and the mainly female staff did not think it was a gentlemanly way to behave at all. Such is nature.

Our staff were a pleasure to work with. Most had been brought up locally and a family atmosphere prevailed. We were a solid team and each helped occasionally with jobs they were not used to. One evening, just before the end of a surgery, only the receptionist and Di, our dispenser, were left in the building when a young lady came in complaining of severe stomach pains. She was quite a big girl, and the pains had been coming and going all day but were getting worse. Di showed her to the Nurses Treatment room and helped her onto the couch before asking me to see her. Examination revealed a lady about to give birth. There was no previous history of pregnancy, indeed this was denied, but although I am not an obstetrician there was no denying my diagnosis. The nearest maternity unit was twenty miles away, the Ambulance would have to get here and then to the Hospital, so we got on with the job. In a few minutes, Di and myself had delivered a healthy boy, dealt with the cord and placenta, and I don't know which of us was the more pleased. The Ambulance arrived a few minutes later and mother and child went off to Hospital.

We performed a bit of minor surgery in the Nurses' room, but most of it was done in the Hospital. I did a lot of manipulation of backs and necks, and various staff helped with that. It usually meant holding onto the far end of a patient who was laying on the couch whilst I pulled and twisted the neck at the other end. I had done a course over some weeks to become proficient with a doctor called James Cyriax, who looked exactly like Alfred Hitchcock and was a bit estranged from main stream medicine, but his methods worked sometimes and I was a fan of physical rather than chemical medicine. Various staff, anyone who was available in fact, acted as anchor man for the procedures, but they had to be vigilant and reasonably powerful when strong traction was applied at the head end. It is difficult to hang onto the legs of a horizontal human, and on several occasions grips were lost and two of the trio landed in a heap at one end! Alternatively, trousers were often separated from their owners, much to the mutual embarrassment of both the non-doctors.

At the Barn Surgery, I had a lovely sign which Lenny Prill, a local artist, had made for me. It was a copy of one seen in Florida when we had taken the family to Disney World, and had been a Wild West doctors' sign. It consisted of a bandaged finger pointing in the direction of the old surgery entrance, and at the bottom of the writing was "Animals doctored when time permits". We were blessed with many good vets in the area, but operating on animals is just the same as humans to me. One good friend bred Standard Schnauzer dogs, but complained bitterly about how much the vets charged to lop their tails. They were not well off, so I decided it was a within my abilities and could be done after hours. I knew my partners would all be aghast at the suggestion, but never mind, they didn't need to know. Six little pups duly arrived at the end of a surgery and the staff all went home. Now vets just lop off the tails, or they did in those days, but I thought that was a bit cruel. Duly each animal was infiltrated with lots of local anaesthetic at the base of the tail, the segment removed under the watchful eye of the owner to exactly the right length, and then some small absorbable sutures applied to close the wound. The dogs were not upset, the owner was delighted, and I wondered how much I could be sued for by my veterinary colleagues. I did do a lot more operating on various animals, but not in the surgery.

Daily work was varied. Whilst the complaints may have sometimes been slightly mundane, the patients were rarely so. It is one of my weaknesses that I believe everyone has a tale to tell, and nobody is boring always. So if an illness was sometimes glossed over and other subjects discussed then I belatedly apologise. One less than interesting complaint was wax in the ears. This is common, a real nuisance to the sufferer, and easy to fix.

Apparently the nurses do most of the ear syringing nowadays, but they are busy people, and it only takes a few moments to perform. I always explained what was going to happen; I would squirt some warm water from a big syringe into the ear, and the wad of wax would be forced out into a kidney dish that the patient held against their head in readiness. As a final command I asked the patient to hold their thumb against the other ear in case I was a bit too energetic and the jet of water went straight through to the other side. Nearly everyone did so until they realised I was joking!

Medical jargon is confusing, sometimes even for doctors. Especially confusing is the names of drugs, which always seem to be long and alike one another. A dear old lady had been to see me a few weeks previously because of sluggishness in her bowels. It was a problem she had had for several years and had no sinister features. After checking her over she was given a medicine called Senakot, which is a natural vegetable laxative. At that time we had some problem with recording our consultations, and when she came back to see me she wanted more of the same medication as it had worked so well. Sadly I had not a record of what she had been given, and she had problems remembering the name. Her head swayed back and forth with the effort of recall, but then she remembered that it began with the letter "S" and the swaying head recommenced. The flash of inspiration on her face made me realise that the drug name had returned. "Semtex" she proudly shouted! Patients had told me in the past that they had "gone like a bomb", but the substance was not part of our dispensary armoury. She was given some more senakot.

Farmers are generally a stoical lot. They rarely come to see the doctor, and only when they have tried, without success, potions that the vet has given for their animals will they attend their GP. It must be a very difficult job, good one year and bad the next, all due to the vagaries of the weather. They work hard, but not perhaps as hard as they think they do. One local farmer was a friend as well as a patient. He was a great sporting man, and fished for salmon in the local river Frome each summer. He spent quite a lot of time in this pursuit, and it surprised me that he could take so much time away from the farm. I questioned him about it. "You, know Rog, that in the winter, I do the work of two men, and so in the summer it is only reasonable to spend a few hours away". This seemed a very reasonable response; all work and no play makes Jack a dull boy. The following winter, however, it seemed that the same farmer was at all the local shoots, on many days of the week. I asked him about it. "You know, Rog, in the summer I do the work of two men, and in the winter it is only reasonable to spend a few hours away". Farmers have a lovely life.

Doctors are not immune to illness. I was very lucky in not having to take one day off work for illness in the thirty years I was in Dorset, but did suffer from the occasional cold. It is not easy to appear calm, relaxed and proficient with a dripping nose, and sniffing or using endless tissues is not attractive either. If I was having a particularly difficult time I would use a nasal spray to limit the offending discharge. It was called Otrivine, and worked very well to dry up the drip, but did tend to cause some blockage if used too much. During one winter surgery I was suffering but working with the aid of the spray. A patient went out, and it gave me the chance to give myself another dose before the next patient came in. In those days we had no intercom, and the next patient came in when the previous went out. There was just enough time to reach into the draw of my desk, grab the spray and dose myself. The problem was that I had lots of other stuff in the drawer. A fumble around, without looking, revealed a spray, and I gave a good dose up one nostril. Oh, the pain! It felt like I had set my nostril on fire, my eyes started to water, the nose continued to drip, and the patient arrived. She was a sensitive young lady who I knew vaguely only, and I tried to hide my distress from her by covering one eye with my hand and absorbing some of the drips from the nose in my palm. I was unable to say much, but she began a long history of a distressing emotional problem, and all I could do was make the occasional nod in her direction. My eyes were streaming even more now, but she finished the consultation by thanking me for being so patient and understanding and left the room. It was only then that I checked the spray to find that I had picked up the Cervical Smear Fixative instead! It is almost pure ethyl alcohol and no wonder my nasal passages had not liked it. A short pause in the surgery was needed for my recovery, but the young lady had chatted to our receptionist on the way our and told her what a lovely doctor I was, because he "actually shed a tear or two" when she told me her problems. If only she knew.

Patients vary in their fear of doctors and in particular fear of injections. For me, being able to immunise a child without the kiddy feeling the needle was a challenge that could be overcome. If the little one is talking, and if I warned them that I was going to press their arm firmly, then by injecting and squeezing at the same time the patient felt nothing. Parents were amazed and I was very proud! But sometimes the pain is in the head. Bill, my friend and helper, had a strapping son called Gary, who was in his late teens, but still terrified of needles, and who tended to faint. He needed a tetanus booster, and Bill asked if he could come in with his son to offer some support. Naturally I agreed. We laid Gary on the couch, as it is quite difficult to faint when laying down. The jab was given, just after Gary had closed his eyes in fear. It was all too much for poor Bill, who fainted and fell unconscious to the floor. It is rare to have a faint in the office, but effectively I had two at the same time! Both eventually came round and made their way slowly from the surgery, supporting each other in a statement of family unity!

We are becoming more and more dissatisfied with our appearance over the years, and the rise of plastic surgery has increased enormously. I used to remover ugly warts and lumps and bumps for patients, but sometimes referrals were made for cosmetic surgery. One very pretty young mother came to see me and somewhat embarrassed, explained that she had always been very self-conscious of her ugly nose. Sally had saved up enough money to have it operated upon and wanted a referral to the local hospital. Her nose looked normal to me, but she could do what she wanted with her hard earned money, and a referral was made. The Consultant Plastic Surgeon was late for his appointments that day, but Sally was asked to wait for him in his consulting room. She paced back and forth and looked in his mirror repeatedly. Perhaps her nose wasn't too bad after all, and she was being vain and silly. At that moment the great man arrived, a bit flustered and keen to get on with his business. Sally looked at this tall man, who possessed the biggest and ugliest nose she had ever had the displeasure to see. She was flushed with embarrassment, overcome by her stupidity, made her excuses and left the consulting room, never to complain about her nose again!

I liked seeing kiddies in the surgery. It was a pleasure when they began to trust the doctor, and would sometimes even sit on my knee to be examined. I doubt if that is allowed now. Sometimes it was the parent who was the patient, and the children had to be quiet whilst mother gave her history. One family came in with a little girl of about five and her two year old brother, whilst mummy came for the consultation. She was starting to tell me her problem when the daughter interrupted to say that "Andrew has got number elevens". We both ignored the little girl, but a few moments later came the louder report that "Andrew has got great big number elevens". We had got to an important part of our conversation and she was again ignored. Finally mothers skirt was pulled, and an even louder shout "Mummy, Andrew has got great big green number elevens". I had, of course, been listening to both conversations, but had no idea what number eleven meant. It was only when we both looked down at little Andrew with his bilateral pustular green nasal discharge that it all became clear! My kids all had number elevens after that.

We had a very efficient and well known gynaecologist who worked locally. His patients included some royalty and patients came from far and wide to see him privately. The mother of one of my patients had come down from the North, especially to see the Consultant, and had stayed with her daughter before her appointment. All went well, the consultation was completed, and, very satisfied that her health was good, she returned to her daughters' house. She was a little puzzled, however, by the specialists' final remark of "and thank you for preparing yourself so thoroughly for me", and asked her daughter what this may have meant. An assessment of hygiene measures before the meeting was made. "What did you wash yourself with Mum?" "Oh I just used the soaps you had in the shower, and then I sprayed myself with that nice preparation in the mauve canister". "But Mum, that was my Disco Glitter!"

Sometimes patients could be less than truthful with the doctor. Old Reg worked at the local garage serving petrol, a stooped man who wore thick glasses and had mild cataracts. He was on the waiting list for operation, but grew impatient. He came to see me complaining that his eyesight was now so bad that he could barely see a thing, and that he needed to be put on the urgent waiting list for operation. I knew he was telling porkies. A couple of days later I was passing the garage in my car. Reg was serving a customer, and I was about fifty yards away when I gave him a cheery wave. Back came the wave from Reg, before he realised what he had done! He rushed over to the car, dodging the traffic, and explained that he knew it was the doctor because he recognised the sound of my car. He did get his operation in the end, but not on the urgent list.

The Practise looked after several local Private Schools. The largest was Bryanston, just over the river from the main surgery in Blandford. Looking after the children at a Public School is not a problem, but dealing with the parents of the pupils often was. It was not a job for me, but luckily my Senior Partner had done it for some time and was very adept. Each year the pupils had an immunisation against the flu'. With several hundred to be dealt with it was quite a task, so all the doctors in the practise came together to form a team of jabbers. The pupils were formed in lines, on line for each doctor, and the whole school could be treated in a couple of hours. We each had our battery of syringes, arms were bared, and skin punctured with accuracy and efficiency. I was dealing with the last of the six rows of pupils, and was surprised when one young man, perhaps not the sharpest tool in the box, presented his arm. It was already bleeding a little, and looked traumatised. Further questioning revealed that he had not understood the instructions properly and had started the morning in the first queue and made his way to the last. I was to be his sixth injection! He is probably in line to become Prime Minister or something now, and I doubt if he has had the flu!

THE TELEPHONE.

I can remember when we first had a telephone at home in Balham. Kelvin 2720 was the number and I was about seven years old. It rang very rarely, but when it did I was scared to death, and it was strange to hear another voice at the other end. How times have changed, with the new phones able to do almost anything except dig the vegetables. Some of my older patients in the villages had the same problems with the phone as I did, and only used the thing when absolutely necessary. Ringing the doctor was only done in an emergency, as business was usually done by leaving notes or attending the open surgeries. The concept of an answerphone was a new one to Okeford Fitzpaine, and caused some confusion when it was first installed. At lunchtime the phone to the dispensary was put on answer only. I had a very irate Trowbridge (one of the extended local families) in the branch surgery in the village one day as he had not been able to renew his prescription. He could not understand why the lady on the other end of the phone would not talk to him, and she even put the phone down at the end of her one way conversation. It was much better when a message could be dropped in a box!

Telephones had been around for some years previously of course. I love the story of one of my predecessors, Dr Richardson, who had a troublesome family to look after in Blandford, several miles away. They used to telephone him for very minor complaints, usually during the night, and would always insist that he attended. Dr Dick always attended, but was a forthright character and longed for some sort of recompense for his troubles. One night he was called for a birth at a village the other side of Blandford. All went well, the baby was delivered, and it was 4am when he began his drive home. On passing through the town, he stopped his car at the house of the troublesome family, hammered on the door, and smiled sweetly when the father appeared bleary eyed to answer. "I was just passing and stopped in case you needed anything, I hope all the family is well". He was not bothered much after that!

Telephone calls must be clear and precise. I often failed. One young lady of the parish came to see me with a delicate vaginal problem. She reassured me that she had never been with a man and remained a virgin, but had some discharge that needed assessment. She was adamant about not having had any sexual encounter. Duly swabs were taken, and sent to the laboratory. Sometimes delays occur in the reporting of results, often with the most anxious of patients for some reason. She rang several times but no results had been received, and the phone was put through from the secretary to myself. Without thinking, and using day to day vernacular, I replied "well there's obviously been a cock up." It was not the response she wanted, and my veracity as a doctor was aggressively questioned. It took a lot of apologies and backtracking to calm the poor girl.

Madeleine was a very attractive ex model, married to a highly successful local businessman. She was known to us socially as well, and kept herself in very good condition. She attended all the well woman clinics, and had her annual mammogram without fail, each year. Again, for some reason her latest result was late. She rang daily to see if it had come, and became a little bit of a nuisance to the staff. Eventually I opened the daily reports to find a normal result. I was a bit pressed, but decided to ring her in between patients, to tell her the good news. Madeleine was a refined lady, with a refined voice, and she answered the phone immediately. "Your breast are perfect, Madeleine". I blurted out. There was a pause at the other end of the phone, and a haughty voice replied "and who is this speaking please!" We have laughed together about it since.

I had a call one day from the Morris Dancing Association. The pursuit is very popular in Dorset, and I admire the dancers very much although I have not participated myself. They were looking for a local doctor to look after the local dancers, and had heard from a patient of mine that I may be suitable for the task. I had too much work already, but because the chap was a neighbour and friend I agreed to help. It wasn't as simple as that though. A form had to be completed to make sure my own medical condition was good. The form duly arrived, and I filled in the questionnaire. It was a long document, and one question I found too intimate and irrelevant. They wanted to know if I had been circumcised. What this had to do with being the medical officer I had no idea, and it annoyed me more than a little. I decided to telephone the Chief Medical Officer of the Morris Dancing Association in Birmingham, and relayed my anger at such a question. The reply was stunning; "Doctor, I would have thought it obvious, we only want complete pricks in the Morris Dancing Association!"

THE FAMILY.

Life at home continued as normal. We all have our own normal, and with four children, one dog, several cats and all the other animals as well as a time consuming job it must have been hectic. It is strange to look back and wonder how we managed, but I only remember the good times, although I guess there must have been some difficult ones. We were blessed with two boys and two girls, all very different in character, and they all now appreciate their country upbringing. Only one ran away from home, and not for too long, so the parenting couldn't have been bad. They all became used to the way of a country doctor however. Although there was a weekend rota in the practice, all the locals knew I was likely to be at home, and often turned up at the front door of the house. I didn't mind, as long as they didn't object to being sewn up in our kitchen with me in my work overalls. The local Hunt passed our way frequently, and one Saturday a very bloody hunter turned up at the house, bleeding profusely from a face wound he had sustained in falling off his mount. Tommy, then about four, answered the door, and came to tell me, without turning a hair, that "there is a bleedin' horseman outside dad". We sewed him up, one daughter took care of his horse, and he went back to chasing foxes. At that time the girls and I all had our own horses, and used to ride out together. One day, again on a supposed weekend off duty, a call came on our private number that a chap in Shroton had a problem. The horses were all saddled and ready to go, so I nipped into the surgery to fetch some kit and we rode over Hambledon Hill to visit him on horseback. It did not take long and the girls waited outside. Ever inquisitive, after we trotted off, I was asked the nature of the urgency. I explained that the gentleman could not pass his urine, and that I had just stuck a tube up his Willy to ease the problem. No further details were sought.

The children became used to the animals, and took them for granted. When we had orphan lambs the girls would warm them by the Aga, and feed them by bottle until they were old enough to manage by themselves. Often a lamb would die, but the children soon appreciated the reality of life and death. Eating our own animals did cause a problem with one daughter, who will not eat lamb to this day.

Riding horses was a good pastime for a father to do with his daughters, although it was not without stress, especially for the father. The ponies were never right! Either they were not fast enough, would not jump, or just didn't behave properly. I was not a good teacher because I usually did not know what I was doing myself. But we did have lots of fun, and I am proud of the photos we have of all three of us going over the same jump in a cross country course. Picking up horse poo from the field was also good training for the girls, but I think that directive was only followed for a matter of days. Anthony Bailey, the local Blacksmith used to come and shoe the horses, and did it just outside the old Barn surgery. The waiting patients used to go outside to watch him in action, and the wafting smell of burning hoof into my consulting room is a lovely memory.

The girls went to pony club camp each year, and on one occasion I was asked to give a talk to the boys and girls about First Aid. The camp was on a farm at Winterbourne Houghton, and the kids, mainly girls, but with a few boys, slept in the barns and generally ran wild. I knew that attention spans would be very limited, and that my talk had to be impressive. We discussed injuries in the hunt, and how to deal with them, especially bleeding wounds. I had managed to obtain some out of date blood from the hospital, and unknown to the audience, packed a bag under a big bandage on a collaborators' leg. She hobbled in and explained that she had fallen and cut her thigh on a branch the same afternoon. There was all round disbelief in the story until she released the blood, the dressing became drenched and blood flowed onto the barn floor. We then had the attention of the audience, although one girl fainted!

The boys were not interested in horses. Too big, too smelly, no brakes, and they need feeding. So we started mountain biking together. Dorset is very hilly and there are some beautiful bridle paths everywhere to cycle on. It was good for Dad to have some exercise as well, although keeping slow enough for the younger of the two was a bit of a trial. He was not an athlete, and after one long afternoon with a posse of boys over the hills, I asked Jimmy what he thought of mountain biking. "Don't like it, not doing it again" I thought we had had a lovely afternoon, a meandering ride to Turnworth and back, and asked for further information. "It is always uphill both ways" he complained, and never came again. They both loved the little motorbike in the field though, and how no bones were broken with the jumps they constructed I have no idea.

In winter we tried to get away for a skiing holiday, but soon the boys decided that skiing was for girls and they wanted to snowboard. There was a dry ski slope near Dorchester, and we went each week to learn the basics. Children learn faster than adults, and I was soon struggling to keep up with them. I soon learned to wear several layers of trousers, as falling on a hard slope is not good for the buttocks. One week a very large bruise was sustained, covering one cheek completely. It is still embarrassing to recall that the following weekend my wife and I attended a very posh black tie party locally, and after the copious alcohol supplied I revealed my injury to the guests. Photos were taken, and I am still expecting some sort of backlash! But we did become fairly proficient at snowboarding, and to go with the picture of doing the jump with the girls, we now have one of the two boys and me doing the same snowboard jump in Steamboat in the Rocky Mountains. Tommy and I later began windsurfing locally, a wonderful pastime, and we also shared a GP 14 sailing dinghy with a colleague, so there was no lack of pastimes!

Linda, my wife, became involved heavily with the local village and other groups we had joined. Being a trained nurse, she was invaluable and much better that me in dealing with some of the problems over the phone. I overheard her talking to a lactating mother who had phoned me for some advice because of her painful and swollen breasts. "What I used to do was get in a warm bath, go on hands and knees, and let them dangle in the water, it always worked for me." Such sensible advice, but not one I would have given; it's not in the textbooks. She was a very relaxed and competent mother, and her only failing in raising the children is that at night, when breast feeding, she did not hear the baby wake, and it was only when her husband got up, retrieved the child and presented it to her that she responded. I used to think that the best thing about breast feeding is that we chaps can't do it, but she proved me wrong. Our first son was born at home, and I have always loved home deliveries; sadly they are not very common now.

I have been able to indulge myself in lots of little building projects over the years. Yew Hedge House needed a porch for the new entrance we had made when dividing the building into two, and so I set about the task. One day Michael Oliver happened to be passing and stopped for a chat. I loved talking to Michael, and learned so much about the locality, some of it true. He was bemoaning the fact that he had an old tractor with the registration number SYD 1. Car number plated were just becoming collectable at that time in the early eighties, and he wanted to sell it. Unfortunately it was not allowed to change a tractor plate to a car, and so it was worthless. He went silent for a few moments, a very unusual happening with Michael, and then suggested, because the prefix RPR was a Dorset assignation, that the plate RPR10R may exist. My name is Roger Prior, and so it would make a very special addition to my car. I explained to Michael that I didn't really want a personal number plate, but it was interesting none the less. Just then, Jeff Lill, one of our local policeman stopped in his car. He had come for a coffee and chat as well, and we included him in the number plate discussion. "Hang on a minute, I'll find out for you." Jeff phoned Blandford Police Station and in a few minutes the call came back that it was on a Bronze Hillman Avenger, owned by a lady who lived in Bridport, and gave us her name and address. All this is illegal now, but these were the days before computers and privacy acts. Under pressure from both of them I agreed to write to the lady. A response came back that I was apparently the third RPRIOR who had been in touch, the car was for sale, and the price was one thousand pounds. Looking at car values, it should have been about eight hundred pounds. I wrote back and thanked her for her prompt response, but that I was a hard up GP, and that I could not justify spending that amount on money on a car. I thought nothing more about it, but a couple of weeks later another letter arrived, saying that the car was still for sale, despite lots of enquiries, and I could have it for nine hundred pounds. I had told all my chums about the car, and all said I should go ahead, and, more importantly, even the wife agreed. I went to Bridport, bought the car, and asked the lady why she had decided to sell it to me. "Oh, lots of those nasty dealers kept trying to buy the car, but I didn't like them. And my father was a GP!" The plate was on my various cars for twenty five years, and it is still on registration to me in the UK. It proved to be a bit of a mixed blessing as lots of people got to know where I was just by noting the number plate. It did prove very useful one day many years later when I was speeding on coming into Sturminster Newton. A traffic policeman suddenly appeared in the road and pointed his radar trap at me. It was a 30mph zone and I was doing about 50mph. No excuse, I thought, and I deserve it. Just then he looked up, saw the number plate, gazed upwards to the heavens and waved me through. It was another patient of mine! I never sped there again.

A PRIVATE AMBULANCE SERVICE.

I had a patient of about my age in Shillingstone who had been in the Ambulance Service for many years. He had grown tired of being employed, and decided to set up his own private enterprise. It was a sensible move, as the number of nursing homes in Dorset were rapidly rising and there was often a call for long distance moves which the NHS could not provide. He bought and converted a big Citroen estate car, advertised widely, and was very successful. Not satisfied, he wanted to expand to being able to include Europe in his trips, and had a friend with a light aircraft who offered to join his enterprise. They needed a Medical Director for the firm, and who better than their GP, who after all had lots of letters after his name, and had been in the Royal Air Force? It all sounded like a lot of fun, so we three became joint directors of the firm, had lots of fancy brochures published, and waited for the work to arrive. The land based vehicle was busy, but we waited some months before the aircraft was needed. It was used for other business in the meantime, so that was not really a problem. A call came for the repatriation of a gentleman who had sustained a severe head injury in Switzerland. His recovery had been slow, he needed oxygen to breath, and would need a doctor to accompany him on his flight. He had been bed ridden for several weeks, and was quite weak. This was the big one, the trip that would really put our firm on the map. Over a few days we managed to convert the rear of the little plane with one stretcher on one side and a seat for the doctor at the patients' head. The oxygen was installed, and we were ready to go. I was very comfortable in the seat at the back, and my colleagues were happy in the front. We took off from the grass airstrip at Compton Abbas airfield and were on our way. Flying a light aircraft is completely different from the airliners we have become used to. They fly much lower, slower, and closer to the ground. It took hours to reach Geneva airport, and I recall my amazement on flying over France at how much wooded area there was. Eventually we landed, and began seeking the ambulance and take over this sick mans' care. No ambulance could be seen. There was one chap with a suitcase by his side, standing patiently on the tarmac and looking a bit lost. We decided to ask him if he had seen an ambulance waiting for an important casualty transfer to the UK. "That's me," he replied, "I've been waiting for an hour for you". It would seem that his condition was not as bad as we had imagined. I interrogated the patient to find that his head injury was much better, and the only problem he now had was that he could not lie flat because it caused him dreadful headaches. On the return trip, oxygen was not needed, the patient sat in the doctors' chair, and the doctor lay on the stretcher! We dropped him off at Gatwick Airport where he was picked up by a family member in an ordinary car. It was good fun though to land in a small plane in a huge airport amongst all the giant airplanes. I can't remember what eventually happened to our firm, but that was the only air ambulance trip I made.

TUMBLEDOWN.

I had a friend from Medical School days, who was initially an orthopaedic technician but later formed his own firm, specialising in supplying medical equipment for films and television. Ron would buy up surplus instruments and kit from closing hospitals for next to nothing, store them in a warehouse, and use them on various film and television sets. He also has lots of older kit for historical programmes. He was a very ebullient and attractive character with a wonderful spontaneous laugh and became well known in the film world. Very sadly, some years later I was called to a local warehouse where Ron kept his props to find him dead from a heart attack. It seems sometimes that it is those who give most to our lives are the ones to go first. Anyway, Ron had been asked to supply the kit for a big BBC film about the Falklands War. It was to be directed by Sir Richard Eyre, and starred a young actor called Colin Firth. They had been looking for someone to act as Medical Advisor for the project; who had some war experience from the forces, and Ron said he knew the perfect person! It was a bit tricky to wangle some leave from the practice, but for two weeks my profession changed to being an advisor to some top theatrical and film personalities. They were lovely! I had never really thought much about making films, and the level of discipline involved, the hours they worked, and the number of times that scenes were repeated was a real lesson to me. I even advised Colin Firth regarding how he acted after being injured in the film, though nobody believes me when I say I was one of his first directors! We filmed at the old Ealing Studios in London, and at the John Radcliffe Hospital in Oxford, and at one point in the film my finger appears on an ophthalmoscope, as the actors had some problem in using the instrument. Linda and I went to the private showing in London, and my chest puffed out when my name appeared in the credits. I was asked to do some more work for the BBC after that, but my life was in Dorset, and I didn't want to change the direction of my career. Variety is the spice of life, however, and it was great to have had that experience.

COUNTRY PURSUITS.

I am a London boy who has always loved the country. I did dangle a rod on the local Tooting Bec Common ponds, but apart from that I knew little about Hunting, Shooting and Fishing. Until I came to Dorset that is. We had the River Stour within a mile, shooting estates all around, and the Portman Hunt just outside Blandford.

FISHING.

I am not sure what it is about fishing. For me it began with visits to my cousins in Surrey, where my uncle Chris taught me and his son Keith how it was all done. A very patient man who spent most of the day untangling our lines. They lived at Addlestone, which to me was the countryside, although it was only twenty miles from us in south London. I remember catching my first fish in the river Wey, and identifying it as a Bleak. My uncle thought I had called a sheep, and for many years after he always asked how many sheep I had caught. But once the fishing bug has caught us, it rarely leaves, and although my trips are rare nowadays, they are always enjoyable. Non fishermen fail to believe us when we say how much we have enjoyed the day when nothing has been caught, but it really is true. Poor little fishes, a great hook stuck in its lips and then either a bash on the head if it is to be eaten, or then chucked back to wait for the wounds to heal. I can't justify it, but love it just the same. It is faintly ridiculous to feel the great excitement we fishermen feel when we have seen a trout feeding, have cast a fly in the right spot, and the fish takes the lure. All that time, money and effort to catch a little fish we could have bought for next to nothing in the supermarket.

We formed a fishing club when I was in Medical School. For some reason it qualified as a sport, and we were given a good grant to start the club and join local groups. The grant was soon exhausted in the Lemon Tree pub, but we did go fishing, both in local rivers and in the sea from Newhaven. I took my fishing rods on one Cricket Tour to Exeter, and one morning boasted about going to the coast to catch some mackerel and bring them back for breakfast. Various bets were made, and I set off with Steve Westaby in my little MGA at some ungodly hour in the morning. Despite all our efforts, no mackerel were about that morning, but we could not possible go back empty handed. It was too early for the shops to be open, but one fellow fisherman, a wily local man, said he had some in his freezer. We agreed to his exorbitant demand for payment, took a half dozen frozen fish from him, and made our way back to Exeter. Frozen fish would have been a bit suspicious, so they were placed next to the car heater on the return journey. On arrival they were nicely defrosted, but smelt a bit old. We were just in time for breakfast, presented our catch to win the bet, only to find that locally caught mackerel was already on the menu for that morning, and all interest in the fish had finis

I had done lots of sea fishing whilst in the RAF, and recall the sunny days in Masirah Island spent in a little fishing boat catching loads of different fish, or casting a rod from the beach and studying on a lounger until I had a bite. But those days were long gone. I had learned how to cast a fly and trout fishing became another pastime. There a lots of pretty trout streams in Dorset and Wiltshire, as well as dedicated Trout Lakes. A huge advantage of being a country GP is that patients often asked me out for a days' fishing on their private water.

I loved fishing with George Crowley. George was a retired Admiral, who had skippered the Royal Yacht Britannia, and had moved to join his family in Dorset. He was a very friendly man, loudly spoken, but short and very rotund. There are lots of Crowleys, and to distinguish him from the others he was known as "Roly Poly" Crowley. Sadly George had a medical condition which interfered with his eyesight, but he drove his car nevertheless. On one occasion we were speeding towards Salisbury along the main road and something came the other way, causing George to swerve somewhat. "Roger", he boomed, "was that a bicycle or a lorry coming the other way?" I insisted on driving after that. We fished a pair of lakes just in Hampshire, often starting very early in the morning. On one particularly beautiful May morning, the sun was just burning off the mist from the perfectly calm surface. I was on one side of the lake and George on the other, and we were the only fishermen present. The sound of our fly lines whooshing through the rod rings and the singing of the birds were the only noises to be heard. All was peace and pure relaxation. "Roger!" A huge voice pierced the calm and even caused some ripples on the water between us. "Roger, do you know the secret of successful fishing?" The calm having been completely shattered, I was slow to reply, but before I could regain my thoughts the answer came loud and clear: "ABSOLUTE SILENCE!" We did not catch any fish that day.

I was lucky enough to fish the rivers Wylie, Allen, Piddle and Frome, all pretty chalk trout streams, and did my very best to preserve the fish stocks by often not catching any. I started to tie my own flies, and caught a wild brown trout on one in an unfished brook only a mile away from our house. How the silly trout could have thought my feathered monstrosity was a fly I do not know, but it was in the spring when the Mayfly are hatching and the period for fishing is known as "Duffers fortnight". Fontmell Brook ran through a patients' farm, and Barney Doble was kind enough to let me fish there whenever I wanted to. I could be fishing within ten minutes of leaving home, all alone in the middle of the Dorset countryside, and felt a very lucky man.

I liked Pike fishing as well, but never caught much. I was explaining my ineptitude to Jerry Broadway, a neighbour, and explained that I would like one to cook and eat, but had not had any success. "No problem, Rog, I'll catch you one and leave it at the surgery for you". Jerry spent a lot of time on the Stour, and had become the local expert. I know the vagaries of fishing and forgot about his promise until about a week later when one of the secretaries implored me to go outside the building and see the "thing" hanging from our Tree of Heaven. There, suspended by its tail, was a six pound pike. I took it home and we made some quenelles. I won't do it again though, too many little bones.

The more we fish, the less we know. I took the boys several times hoping they would catch the fishing bug as well. They didn't. Maybe it was all too easy for them. We went to a patients' pond in Shillingstone to try and catch some carp. Jimmy, my youngest, was faffing about with his line just in the water near the bank. I informed him of the errors of his ways and that there was no chance of him catching anything there, just at the moment when his rod was nearly pulled from his hand by a six pound carp! No wonder he didn't listen to me anymore. I even took them night fishing on the Stour once. It was a big adventure, the two boys in their tent and me and Finnegan the dog in the other, camping on the bank in a farmers' field. All I remember was no fish, constant whingeing, and that sleeping with a boxer dog is not a good idea. The odours emitted from that animal had to be endured to be believed. We never did it again.

I did do some Salmon fishing on the Frome, on a stretch which was rented by farmer Austin Lukins. I have never caught a salmon, and was unlikely to do so there. Austin was a good fisherman, and he hadn't caught any that year either, so there was no chance for me. But one of the charms of fishing is the environment, seeing the flora and fauna, and being in good company. I have never fished with someone I didn't like, and maybe that is another charm of the sport, we can all commiserate and all celebrate with understanding. There were several well-known anglers amongst my patients, and the only problem with that is they rarely were allowed to discuss their medical problems until the latest fishing stories were discussed. Here in France we have a lovely large local river, the Creuse. Each year I buy a permit to fish, and each year I do go once or twice only, and have yet to catch anything worth catching. And each year I tell myself I will go more often the following year. Such is the lure of fishing.

SHOOTING.

When I was at Battersea Grammar School, I was in the Combined Cadet Force. I proudly attained the position of Lance Corporal, and did a lot of stamping about in the Drill Squad. And during our training on various Army camps, we shot Enfield 303s and Bren guns. Not at each other, but at targets. It was the only shooting I had done.

In Dorset shooting is one of the main country pursuits. The only interest I had in it was that the thousands of Pheasants that were released each year tended to attack the wheels of my car when I was on my rounds. How many thousand are killed each year by passing traffic I am not sure, but it must be a good proportion of the birds raised.

I had a wealthy gentleman patient with an incurable cancer who lived in a very pretty converted mill at Fontmell Magna. His pain was well controlled, his caring wife looked after him, and there was very little medical care needed. I visited him often, and we talked about life in general. We had both been in the Air Force, and reminisced together. Over the weeks, he became very weak, and most of the talking came from my side. I told him about the geese we had lost to the fox the previous week, and he nodded knowingly. He died a few days later. His wife came to see me a week or two afterwards, and brought with her a big package. It was one of his old shotguns. He wanted the Doctor to have it to try and shoot the fox. I was very touched, and it became my prized possession. It was side by side double barrelled gun made in Birmingham in 1911, with a beautiful walnut stock and wonderful engraving. The one instruction that came with it was that I had to learn to use it! The first thing of course, is to apply for a licence, and the Police were very diligent in making sure that I was not a potential bank robber and that the gun would used for sport only. The licence had to be renewed each year, which I often forgot, and one year a local bobby turned up at the front door to tell my wife that he had come to arrest her husband because he had an unlicensed gun! He was joking of course and had only come for a cup of tea, but the wife was convinced for a moment.

Having a shotgun is the first step, but then it is necessary to learn how to use it. Ron Doble, a retired farmer, and father of friend Barney, held regular clay pigeon shoots on the farm, and asked me along. He didn't know that I was a complete novice, but I had bought the cartridges and a belt and thought I looked quite professional. Clay pigeons are little saucer shaped targets which are slung out of a launcher and fly for a few hundred metres through the air. Sometimes two are slung out at the same time, and the aim is, obviously, to shoot them down. I watched the other chaps have a go and it looked easy. Not so for me. There was lots of Dorset chuckling when the doctor missed clay after clay, but after admitting to being a novice, lots of helpful advice was given and, to the applause of the dozen or so guns, I actually hit one. It improved a lot after that and we had several very enjoyable mornings on the farm.

But clay pigeon shooting is very different from shooting flying birds. Clay pigeons slow down after they are slung in the air, but birds accelerate.

And completely different is shooting rabbits. Steve Bryant ran a little farm at Fontmell Parva, and invited me for an evenings' rabbit shooting. Rabbits had become very common in Dorset and were becoming a nuisance, eating the early crops. They taste good as well, so I had no moral objections to joining him. They are not easy to hit, and are very wary, coming out at dusk, and bolting at the slightest noise. The technique was to use a bright lamp to pick them out and then shoot before they could move. We managed about a dozen between us, but then all rabbits in the area got the message and scarpered. Can't blame them.

The paying shoots in Dorset are Big Business affairs. Each estate will have a Gamekeeper, or sometimes two, and very many thousands of pheasants and partridge are raised over the summer for release in the Autumn when the shooting begins. These are Driven Shoots, which means a band of beaters walks in a row through the estate towards a waiting line of shooters, making noises and bashing the undergrowth with sticks so that the birds take fright and fly over the waiting guns. The location on the estate is changed several times during the day, and each beat is called a drive. The sport is the skill involved in shooting sometimes high and fast flying targets. Lots are killed, and more are missed by the guns. The rolling hills and valleys of Dorset provide an excellent environment for sporting shooters, and clients come from all over Britain and the Continent. It costs a fortune for one days' shooting, but a brace of pheasants is the only tangible reward. There is a line of shoot lovers with their dogs waiting behind the gun line to pick up the dead birds and to chase down the injured ones. Being a picker up is a skill in itself, and the dogs have to be well trained and disciplined. It is a sport where one's ability is watched by both the guns and the picker uppers, and misses and good shots will be well recounted later.

We were surrounded by big shooting Estates in Child Okeford. I joined the beaters on several occasions, as I knew the gamekeepers well, and it was a lot of fun as well as an insight into the antiquated arrangements for masters and employees. At lunchtime the guns would all go off to the Great House and have a slap up lunch for an hour or two. The beaters were sent to a barn to sit on straw bales and eat their sandwiches, and if lucky, drink a beer sent down from the main house. Then, well refreshed, the drives began again in the afternoon. It was all very good natured and the beating team always gave a frank account of the performance of the paying guests whilst slurping the drinks.

Eventually I guess the word got about that the doctor now knew how to handle a shotgun. I was invited to shoot in all the Grand Estates and had a very privileged and enjoyable time. The Estate owners were all patients, as were the gamekeepers, and I usually knew some of the guns as well. The farmers who had their own shoots tended to ask other owners to join them, and the invitations were reciprocated. I was rarely asked for the serious paid days when guests from all over would arrive in their big cars and be lavishly entertained, but the birds were the same and the drives similar. It was a big challenge for the gamekeeper to make sure enough birds were driven for the expensive shoots, and if they did well tips flowed in abundance. My tip was to tell the gamekeeper to drink less beer.

Ranston Estate was magnificent. I shot one day when Selena Gibson Fleming was in her prime and strutting regally about the place and giving advice. She was the widow of the original owner, was very tall, well-groomed, loud, and a commanding figure. The estate held many thousands of pheasants and some partridge, both red legged and the grey variety. The latter are quite rare now, fly fast, and are a prize to shoot. James Gibson Fleming, her son, was nominally In charge of the shoot, and Ernie Brown the very able gamekeeper, but all was under the looming presence of the matriarch. I was on the end of the line of guns one frosty December morning. We had not shot many birds and were all feeling a little chilly. Suddenly a flock of partridge came over my end of the line. They were the elusive grey partridge and flying fast; the game shooters dream. BANG, BANG, I emptied both barrels. And missed them all. There was a horrible pause, and then the feared, loud, expected reprimand from the lady. "Doctor, I have stomped half way across Dorset to get those blasted birds over your gun, and you have just missed the bloody lot!" I don't think I was ever forgiven, and felt like a naughty schoolboy who had spilt ink all over his workbook. I was not asked to an official shoot there again, but James had a much more relaxed approach. One day I was jogging with the dog over Hambledon Hill, to find the shoot on the Shroton side. James saw me puffing and panting in my running gear, and called me over. Giving me his gun, at the end of the line again, he told me that the next drive was about to come over and I could see if my shot had improved. I was sweaty and a little embarrassed to be with the country gentry dressed as I was, but had no time to reflect when the flight of pheasants came over. I missed. Again. "Better stick to doctoring" was the only advice I received.

Peter Hunt and Angus Campbell shared a shoot on the side of Fontmell Hill and in the vale where Peter farmed. He had recently created a pond and for the first time our morning shoot on the hillside would be complemented by a duck shoot in the afternoon. Lunch went well, and we were all looking forward to some sport with the ducks. Peter was quietly proud of his pond and had been feeding the birds to make sure they were around when we were. He explained that they were wild birds and would spook easily and unless we were very quiet in our approach they would all fly off and the sport be lost. Fuelled by the contentment that good food and alcohol can bring, we made our way to the vale, and after whispered instructions from Peter, we formed a large circle around the pond and made our way towards the water. No birds appeared. We were at the raised bankside now, and the whispered command was that Peter would show himself and the duck would all take off and we should be ready for some good shots. He stood up. The ducks swam to the middle of the water and swam around in circles. A bit embarrassed now, our host shouted some obscenities at the birds, but they refused to take off. "Don't worry chaps, I'll put the dogs in". Two of the black Labradors were commanded to take to the water after the birds, and did so with great relish. Dogs can swim well, but not as well as ducks, and there then ensued a procession of a couple of dozen mallard being poorly chased by two rapidly tiring dogs. We could all see the funny side of the situation now, but tried to hold our laughter to ourselves for fear of upsetting the now furious Peter. "Right, I'm sorry chaps, but the only thing to do is to get them up by throwing stones at them. Roger, you play lots of cricket for the village team, come and throw some stones for the other guns". I picked up a handful of pebbles and lobbed one in behind the ducks. No reaction. "Can't you throw a bit closer to them, Rog?" He was a bit desperate now, and I picked up a large stone and threw as hard as I could at the flock. The poor mallard at the rear was hit on the back of the head and killed instantly. One of the Labradors picked the bird up and brought it to the feet of its master. We could not contain ourselves any longer, and mirth replaced the hard held serious faces of the previous minutes. To his credit, even Peter saw the funny side. It was the only duck we killed that day, and was given to me as a prize for the best shot!

Over the years I was lucky enough to shoot on most of the surrounding estates. There are so many facets to the sport, one of them rough shooting with various pals. Basically this involves walking up and down the hedgerows, usually with a dog, and shooting whatever appears. It is a much more relaxed way of shooting; one is always on the move, and the bag is always for the pot. Game birds, pigeons, rabbits and occasionally hares were encountered, and sometimes despatched. It is the way most shooting is done here in France, and to my mind much more defendable. If meat is eaten, then animals have to be killed. When they are taken for the kitchen I can defend it.

My last shooting was at another beautiful estate at Iwerne Minster. The owner was a very wealthy man who did everything to excess. He was very generous, and loved having friends to experience his opulent life. We arrived on a very wet nasty morning and a couple of guests failed to arrive. Seven of us shot 277 pheasant that day, and we finished early because of the weather. To me it was not sport at all. The beaters had been well paid and were wet but happy. The gamekeeper had done his job well, and he was content. The owner was proud that his shoot had killed so many birds. I wasn't. To me it was wholesale slaughter, the flights of birds were so thick that just aiming wildly into the air would kill a pheasant. The sight of the dead birds put me off that sort of shooting. I have no objection to others enjoying their sport, and it is a pleasant social occasion, but I just don't want to kill animals for sport any more. In those days the huge bags could not easily be disposed of for eating, and were sometimes thrown into pits and buried. Indefensible, and less common now I am assured.

HUNTING.

The idea of a group of well off adults dressing up in fine clothes, riding a horse and hunting a fox, aided by a hoard of baying dogs sounds faintly ridiculous. It is. And to ride over prime farming land with all the consequent damage is almost hooliganism. But in those days it was legalised hooliganism and I loved it. We have become embroiled in the rights and wrongs of hunting, and each pole of opinion has its passionate adherents. To me, having lost ducks, geese, chickens and lambs to the fox, he is an enemy of the animal keeper and needs to be controlled. Whether hunting him in the "sporting" fashion is the best way of control I don't know, but it has given lots of pleasure to many generations of country folk. And it is not just for the rich; many riders spend all their spare money on keeping a horse and joining the local Hunt. It is followed by dozens more on foot, bicycle, motorbike   and car and gives enjoyment to thousands in the depths of winter. Often the fox will escape the hunters, and I can recall on a couple of occasions seeing him, whilst on my rounds, trotting unconcerned over the fields in the opposite direction to the hounds and huntsmen. Fit and healthy foxes usually escape the Hunt. There seems to be something objectionable to some, about well-groomed and dressed people on shining horses. Maybe it is that they are high above their observers and seem in some way to appear superior and aloof. On occasions some hunters can be aloof and superior, but they are in the minority in my experience. Taking a glass of sherry or sloe gin, with a mince pie, before the start of the day also alludes to affluence, especially when taken in the centre of the local market town. But in Dorset the Hunt was a valued diversion and firmly a part of the local culture. The local countryside is ideal for hunting, with lots of big fields to gallop over, and lots of hedges to jump, some of them very large. The thrill of following an often uncontrolled herd of excited horses over hill and vale, jumping hedges at top speed is something to be experienced. Pure legalised hooliganism.

The Portman Hunt was our local group. I had the good fortune to know many of the leading lights, and looked after a couple of the Masters of the Hunt. The Master was often a well off knob with no profession and little else to do, and the Hunts seem to transfer these interesting gentlemen between themselves a little like gentrified football managers. But sometimes a local farmer or businessman was the boss for a season or two, and the morale of the group was very much reflected by the leadership. I had not even sat on a horse when I arrived in Dorset, but after learning to ride I was invited to take a day or two with the Hunt. My only experience before had been to attend one of the riders who had been injured after falling off attempting a large jump. There was a Doctor in the field, and the call went round for the Doctor to come and rescue the crumpled figure at the bottom of the ditch. He could not be found. It was only when the prostrate figure was identified that it was the medical man himself who had fallen. I saw him on my rounds a few minutes later; he was badly bruised and may have been knocked out, but, typical of the Hunting type, refused all treatment and was determined to get back on his horse for fear of missing the rest of the day.

So it was with some trepidation that I rode out to my first meeting at Hayes Farm. My horse, Boozer, was an old Hunter loaned to me by Jack Hooper, a well-known local farmer and renowned horseman. The old horse had hunted for many years, but unknown to me, had been rejected by Jack because he now refused to jump! I had borrowed a hunting jacket, polished my boots and tied the faintly ridiculous cravat around my neck. At the reception, I tried to look competent and took my sherry without problem, chatting knowingly with the other members of the hunt in the farmyard. I had not noticed the electric fence behind me. Boozer, for some reason, began walking backwards and his ample buttocks touched the wire. It is difficult to maintain an air of competence, let alone a fine glass of sherry, when an animal is electrocuted. In mid-sentence I was propelled into the air and landed across the animal covered in sticky sherry all over my pristine riding jodhpurs. Much mirth from the on looking professionals, and not a good start to the day. Boozer, however, seemed to be given a new lease of life by the shock, and was difficult to hold back when the hunt actually started. I do not remember all that much about my first day, but know that I fell off several times until told about the fact that the horse had retired from jumping fences. After that we went through gates instead. Boozer had been used on the farm to help round up the cattle, and could open a gate almost by himself. I was determined to stay to the end of the day, but found all the excitement hugely exhausting. Towards the end we all stopped for some reason, and I recall slipping slowly from the saddle due entirely to fatigue. Interestingly, it is common for riders to leave the hunt at any time in the day, and it is customary to say "Good Night Master" to the boss, no matter what time it is. And the fox is known as "Charlie", so if one is seen by a member of the Hunt the call has to be given of "aye aye Charlie" at the top of ones' voice. All a bit strange. The pristine appearance of the Hunt at the start of the day is a little different at the end. Galloping through the winter mud of the Blackmoor Vale for several hours is not a clean pursuit, and the spattering of mud on the riders and horses is taken as a badge of honour. On that first day I did see the hounds kill a fox. Suffice to say that death for the animal is very very quick and certain, certainly quicker than the fox killing my lambs. It looks barbaric, but is probably better than a slow death from an inaccurate bullet or gunshot wound. I could do without the custom of "blooding" a new recruit to the Hunt by smearing the blood of the fox onto the cheek of the hunter, and refused to have it done myself. I only hunted a few times during my career, but enjoyed it immensely. The ban on foxhunting has perversely improved the pursuit locally. Hunting by following a scent trail left by a hunt servant is not the same as the pre ban days, but anti hunt protesters are not seen, and sometimes the hounds chase the fox rather than the trail. In effect little has changed but more people are happy. That can't be bad.

THE ANIMALS.

When I was a nipper in London there weren't many animals about. The odd dog and cat, and sometimes I saw horses from the local stables on Tooting Bec Common. I always wanted to have a budgerigar, but it never materialised for some reason. Maybe I had a subconscious sense of missing something, as life in Dorset was surrounded by animals of all shapes and sizes. In general they are expensive, often noisy, frequently filthy, time consuming, have a tendency to die, and are hugely enjoyable. I guess we love them because they are dependent on us, are usually pleased to see us, and above all are intellectually undemanding and non-judgemental. I can't imagine living without animals now.

DOGS.

As a child I was scared of dogs. I don't know why, as I was never bitten or attacked, but they always seemed to have big teeth and sometimes growled at me. But once we were settled in Dorset a dog was the first animal we considered, but what breed? I wanted a Great Dane, because they are magnificent looking animals, but with a calm temperament. It was not allowed by the Boss, because they are just too big and she would not be able to hold onto it. After some discussion we decided to buy a Boxer. They are funny to look at, good with children and able to play with Dad as well. Joyce Malcolm was a local breeder at Winterbourne Clenston, and we made an appointment to see her. Dog breeders are a particular group, passionate about their chosen breed, and all with a potential champion dog. I didn't want a champion dog. All that poncing about at Crufts has always seemed a pointless exercise to me, and only seems to serve to increase the selling price of the puppies. Anyhow, Joyce just happened to have a litter, and one of them was very ugly because half of its face was white and it would never make a show dog. Perfect. We bought him for the very knock down price of £60. The next problem with a dog is what to call him. Being a boxer, and having boxed myself at school, I followed the sport closely, and at that time the local hero of British boxing was Henry Cooper. My mothers' maiden name was Cooper, and so that was it, the little pup was to be called Henry Cooper. My two daughters loved him, and he was smothered in girly kisses for weeks. Training a dog was a new skill to be learned, but the advantage of my job is that there is always advice to be had from patients, again most of it contradictory! One of the warnings I was given was about the number of Ticks found in our area. They are dropped by the deer, and can cause problems for dogs and for humans. They bite into the skin, suck blood, expand, and eventually drop off. I was vigilant for the little beasts, and one evening when the dog was laying on his back I saw my first tick. It is important to remove the whole parasite, and I vigorously scraped the thing with my fingernail. It would not budge, and then I saw another on the other side of Henrys' belly. That one would not move either. My anatomical training at last kicked in; I was trying to remover the poor dogs' nipples! I will not forget the strange look he gave me. Despite that, he turned into a fine animal, always ready for a romp with his master, and always gentle with the girls, but he was very ugly and tended to slobber a lot. I loved him, and he would always come with me on my rounds.

Soon after we acquired the dog I finished building my kit car. It was made from the mechanics of an old MGB that I bought for £120 and a body made by a chap called Nick Green on the south coast. It looked like a pre-war Aston Martin, with an open top and I was very proud of it. The work had taken many months, and had a dashboard made from an old bed head and it was lined with surplus carpet. I still have it today, and it is still widely admired here in France although falling apart. The day arrived for the first test drive on the road. Naturally the dog wanted to come with me, so was sat upright in the one passenger seat. It was a cloudless spring day, the birds were singing, the cow parsley lined the lanes and I was in Heaven with my faithful dog beside me. After a mile or so, catastrophe, a water leak had developed and droplets were flying into my face. I stopped the car and opened the bonnet to find the leak. All seemed well so we drove on, a little puzzled. The droplets still wetted my face, but, it seemed, only on the left side. I looked at Henry and found the cause of the problem; his jowls were flapping in the breeze and propelling his saliva all around the car! But much better that than a failure of my mechanics, and I soon got used to the involuntary shower each time I used the vehicle. The Boxer came with me every day the open top was used. He was normally a placid animal, but very protective of the vehicle, and growled at anyone stopping to talk to him if I was not beside him. It was because of that behaviour Gillie spread the rumour about his amputated arm being stolen.

I loved the car so much, and the dog loved the car so much, that when winter came we still wanted to use it, despite the inclement weather. I found an old Army Surplus anorak which suited him perfectly. The body was zipped up, the arms tied around Henrys' chest and the hood raised over his head. He was comfortable and happy, and we spent many winter days doing my calls together. One evening, our lovely Practice Nurse, Kay, rather bashfully said she needed to talk to me after my surgery was finished. I guessed she had some sort of personal problem, but it was more serious than that. There was local gossip that the Doctor had a mistress. He had been seen driving his open car around with a blond woman wearing an anorak! I was flabbergasted. Not by the rumour, but by the fact that I would have chosen an ugly male dog with a half white face and flapping jowls as an alternative to my lovely wife.

We had some narrow and winding lanes in Dorset. Locally a corner is known as Steepleton Bends, and Henry soon got used to leaning over for the corner, which I often took as fast as I could. One day we were coming back for lunch and I was screaming round the corner, tyres screeching, as normal. The dog was leaning over almost onto my lap, and the old car was roaring beautifully round the bend. But then, coming the other way, was a policeman on a motorcycle. I saw him stop just round the bend and begin to follow me. Bugger, I thought, I don't want to get caught for dangerous driving. I knew the way back home very well indeed, and hoped he didn't, so put my foot down as hard as I dared. No sign of the motorbike, we must have lost him. I roared through out village, and pulled into the drive, blessing my close escape. It was not to be, a large Policeman pulled into the drive behind me. Fair cop, I reckoned, he must have been speeding as well to catch me. "Bloody Hell Rog, I was only stopping to show you the new BMW, I didn't realise that old bus could go so fast!" It was Andy, one of my patients who had recently transferred to the Traffic Police, and was very proud of his own plaything. He came in and had lunch with us.

Boxers are not the most intelligent of dogs. To my mind that is a good thing, as I think a Collie would be brighter than I am. Henry could not count. I found this out one day whilst taking him for a walk in the surrounding fields. Gilbert Ransome, a local Hunting man, was out walking his two rather pugnacious Jack Russel dogs. They were from the same litter and looked similar. One dog was in the bushes as we walked past, and the other rushed up to Henry and tried to attack him. I don't know why, but small dogs, especially terriers, seem to attack bigger dogs, maybe because they are scared of them. Anyway, Henry did not think this little thing was worth scrapping with, and merely pinned it to the ground with one paw. It was then that the other Jack Russel came out of the bush and bit Henry on the bum. The first dog was released, the second pinned to the ground with a paw, only for the original dog to bite his backside from the other side! This scenario continued for several repetitions, and the look of utter confusion on the Boxers' face sent Gilbert and I into fits of laughter. Henry was always wary of Jack Russels after that.

Boxers are not long lived dogs. Henry died at six and we were all heartbroken. He may have picked up some poison, and died very quickly. I buried him in the front garden, a tear dropping with each spade of earth I removed. We had the two boys by then as well, and have a beautiful family photograph of us all with our adored Boxer dog.

I don't know the best way to react to the death of a loved pet. We bought another Boxer, this time named after Frank Bruno. He was a fine looking animal and just as faithful as Henry. He also loved the cars, and jumped in at every opportunity, whether he was wanted or not. At that time I had an old BMW as the main practice car, and it often needed topping up with oil. As before, Bruno was not the sharpest tool in the box, and one day, after a long journey, I opened the bonnet to re- fill the oil. Boxers do not know the difference between a boot and a bonnet, and he jumped in enthusiastically. The engine was still hot, and I have never seen a dog jump so high or so rapidly as Bruno making his escape. He never jumped into the engine bay again.

Like humans, some dogs seem to produce more gaseous effluent from their rear ends than others. Bruno was a champion in that respect and could clear a room in seconds. Diet made no difference, and it seemed to happen particularly when he was asleep. Sometimes the release of the gas was accompanied by a very loud noise, which would wake the dog from his slumber. It was the only time I saw Bruno frightened, and he would jump up and look around for where the eruption had come from. We never did cure him, and never took him to dinner parties.

Walking the dog is one of the pleasures of life. It is the perfect excuse for being non -productive, and time for reflection on the joys of existence. I have often wondered what goes through a dogs' mind on those walks; information gained by the nose must be very different from our information. And the way dogs react to one another is a mirror of human behaviour as well, apart from bottom sniffing of course. I began running for exercise when we had Bruno, and although he found it easy to keep up with my ambling pace, it was always imperative to stop and sniff at seemingly random points. I would love to be able to translate the scents he was investigating.

Bruno himself lasted longer than Henry, and we mated him with a pretty Boxer bitch belonging to the wife of a patient. As was the custom, we could have the pick of the litter rather than the owner paying a fee, and we chose a dog we called Finnegan, after Chris, the champion boxer. Bruno lasted a year or so longer, and it was great fun to have the two dogs together.

Boxers are sometimes seen as fierce dogs, but they are completely the opposite in my experience. As with all breeds, it depends on the training and upbringing, but for the laughs they give, and the gentleness with children, they are hard to beat. Daft, durable, and adorable dogs.

I had one very memorable dog experiences when I was attending a Horse Trial as the Medical Officer. For once the humans behaved themselves, and there was very little trauma to be dealt with. Not so with the canine attendees. The local vets were also supposed to be in attendance, but after being called over the Tannoy system, nobody appeared. They must have gone home for lunch. The next best thing to a Vet is a Doctor, and after increasingly frantic calls I was asked to attend the Red Cross Ambulance. A dog had been kicked by a horse. It was a very big horse, and a very little dog, a Chiwawa. The hugely made up lady owner was distraught; her little dog had been running behind the stables, and had been propelled several yards by a flailing hind hoof. It was a very dead dog. No amount of explanation to the lady could convince her of the diagnosis, and she was becoming out of control. I had to respond to her pleas to "DO SOMETHING!" I am not a vet, but reckoned the basic resuscitation techniques for humans may be worth trying. I blew gently onto the little corpses' nose, and then a little more forcefully into its mouth, whilst tapping over its heart region. The dead animal gave a little, involuntary and unwanted twitch. "Carry on, carry on" the lady shrieked, "She's coming back to life!" No way was the little thing coming back to life, but I felt compelled to carry on and blew a little harder. The air I was introducing must have traversed the alimentary canal, because the result of my attentions was a little doggy fart. "You're winning Doctor, do some more like that". The façade went on for several minutes with no further physical effects, and eventually even the painted lady accepted the loss of the little Chiwawa. She was very grateful though, and thought I should retrain for the Veterinary Service. Fat chance of that.

Today in France we are in the process of trying to train our latest puppy, an Airedale. She was bought to try and revive our older dog of the same breed. The puddles and packets left all over the floor are a challenge, but we will get her sorted our eventually. I can't imagine living without a canine companion now. They provide an emotional comfort that does not depend upon the vagaries of how we act or what we say; they seem content just to be fed and to be with us, without questions. They are true friends.

HORSES.

On arrival in Dorset the only contact I had had with horses was to see them from afar whilst playing on our local common in London as a boy. They were great big lolloping things that made strange noises from their nostrils, and stopped to leave great piles of poo. I remember in London that the old rag and bone man had a horse and cart, and if it left a pile in the road there would be a scramble of residents with a shovel to remove the effluent for the garden roses. But Dorset has lots of horses, some used for hunting, some for pleasure riding and some just as pets. My two girls longed to learn to ride and to have a pony each, especially as some of their friends were riders. There are not many things a Dad can do with daughters; they were not keen on soccer or fighting, and fishing and cycling were not to their tastes. So I agreed that they could learn to ride as long as their father learnt with them. With great excitement we booked lessons with Marcia and Geoff Coombes at Bushes Farm. Marcia was a good teacher in the little school, but I shall never forget the first time I sat on the great animal (actually it was little more than a pony) and was given these little bits of leather, called the reins, to hold onto and with which I was supposed to have control. No brakes, and the accelerator was my feet dangling in the stirrups. Luckily, the old horse had done this a thousand times before, and was in automatic pilot mode. Our first lessons consisted of walking around the enclosed arena and trying to sit upright and feel in control. I didn't feel in control. Naturally the girls, being younger, more adept and more supple, found it all very easy and even wanted to trot and then canter the ponies. I wanted to stay in first gear, but was made to increase my speed to the extent that it felt like each part of my body was moving in a different direction. Over the weeks competence did improve, and the time came when we were allowed to venture out from the enclosed area into the great outside world. I was nervous, no brakes, dodgy accelerator which I had heard sometimes gets stuck in the on position, and occasional cars on the road. I am convinced that horses know when one is nervous, and have their own little laughs by making us look and feel ridiculous. So it was with me, when Seamus, an old nag who should have known better, took off with me on a farm track. Hanging onto his neck for dear life and imagining the broken bones when I was going to fall off was a terrifying experience, but he eventually came to a halt at the top of a hill. One thing I have found about horsey people is that they find anything that causes distress to another rider to be hugely amusing. On trying to catch my breath and regaining my composure, Geoffrey came alongside smirking and remarked casually "Oh I forgot to tell you that Seamus always does that here." The daughters thought it was hilarious, of course, and could not wait to tell all their friends about their useless father. But slowly, slowly, confidence came and also some degree of competence. Progression was made to the bigger animals and even some jumping was done in the arena. I remember well someone telling me that it was necessary to fall off at least seven times before one could ride. I stopped counting at twenty!

We had the field at the back of the house at Yew Hedge House, and some old brick built stables. In older times the Doctor would have done his rounds on his horse, and as I was the seventh generation of medical occupant, they had seen some use in the past. They were not in good condition, but even had a farriers' room and the old hooks for hanging bridles and saddles were still in place. It is funny how normally lazy girls can become supercharged when the possibility of owning their own ponies becomes a possibility. In no time the building was in shape and was only missing the equine occupants. The provenance of our first ponies I don't remember, but one was rescued from the knackers' yard, and another was, I think, loaned to by the daughter of a colleague in the next village. They were not good enough! No child has a pony which is good enough. Either they will not jump, will not go fast enough, or go too fast. And some of them bite the owner. No mention is ever made of the possibility that the rider is not of sufficient competence to control the animal; it is always the poor horses' fault. Nevertheless the girls did well on their ponies, aided by attendance at the local Pony Club Camps. The field was big enough for the ponies, as well as the sheep and goat, but horses are not good for the land and tend to destroy the grazing. It is important to pick up their droppings, and this was done by the girls with enthusiasm initially but with more reluctance as the weeks went by. They were leaving Dad behind with their new skills, so I needed to have a horse myself. Casual equine enquiries after prostate consultations with older farmers was a good bet, and sure enough, after a couple of weeks, an old hunter was loaned by Jack Hooper. His name was also Seamus, and he taught me to ride. There is no substitute for learning without an instructor and just feeling how the animal reacts. Seamus took me over the hills and vales of our local countryside, opened gates for me, and even had the occasional sedate gallop. It was only when I build a couple of jumps in our field that I found his fault that he had retired from jumping. I discovered later that Jack had been with the Hunt and found himself in an unusual environment with the Field having to jump a large hedge to follow the Hounds. Seamus refused to jump, disgraced the owner, and had never jumped since that time. I wished he had told me. Having fallen off multiple times with the old horse stopping before the jump, I asked several friends over to show me how it is done. None of them could make him leave the ground. Horses can be stubborn creatures! It did mean, however, that the girls and I could go out riding together, and looking back, it was one of the highlights of Dorset life. The wife was not keen on horses, so it meant some time alone with the girls, which was nice, and it was fortuitous as well, as keeping and shoeing four horses would have broken the bank. Poor old Seamus became slower and slower, and I became keener and keener. It was time to buy a proper horse. Contacts in the horsey world put me In touch with a farmer on the coast who was selling his old Point to Point racehorse. He was past his best, the horse that is, but would still jump and loved to hunt. He was called Pharoes' Gold. Buying horses is a bit like buying used cars, fraught with swindlers, but patients rarely try to fool their doctor in my experience, perhaps in fear of what may happen in the future! I was reassured that he was a good bargain, so we took him home. He drank lots, and rather than adopt his racing name we called him Boozer. I learned to jump on Boozer, and he taught me well. As a child, body position seems to come naturally when jumping, but not so for the older man. It is important to sit upright over jumps rather than to lean forward as is natural. I learnt this doing a Cross Country course at the Hunter Trials at Piddlehinton. These courses are held regularly in Dorset, and consist of multiple and varied jumps, usually through woods and fields, and are a training ground both for the horses and the riders. We, the girls and me, did several together. Some jumps are on the flat, some uphill, and some downhill. The latter are "drop" fences, meaning that the level on the far side is lower than the near. I was progressing round the course rather well, I thought, until we came to my first drop fence. Boozer had done it all before, of course, and was leading me round with his usual nonchalance, and I leant nicely forward over the jump. Big mistake! Leaning forward when the horse is going downhill over a jump is not a stable position, and I was dumped in a heap, bashing my nose on the ground. Each fence is attended by a horsey person. Ignoring my dripping blood, I was advised "You silly arse, don't you know how to jump?" Another example of the understanding support given by riding people to one another. The next step up from the Hunter Trials was the Team Chase. Basically this consists of a race around a cross country course but in teams of four horses and riders. It is very dangerous, and riders often fall off, so the time of the third to arrive is the time for the team. I was asked to become the fourth member of a local team, at the last minute, as one of the others had been taken ill. It was known that I rode an ex racehorse and it was wrongly assumed that I could ride well enough to join them. There was not time enough for me to walk the course beforehand, but I knew where the first fence was and we took off at top speed. Old Boozer had the wind in his tail and led the field at a great and completely uncontrolled gallop. The first fence appeared and I held on for dear life. We flew through the air in a magnificent jump and galloped on straight ahead. "Wow, this is wonderful "I thought, and was still in front of the others. Strange that I could not hear them though, they can't be that slow, or can they? A dangerous glance behind revealed an empty field! And more confusingly I could not see the second fence anywhere. I managed to pull Boozer to a trot and turned around. I should have changed direction left after the first fence! I could just make out the other three riders in the far distance. I was not invited to Team Trial again.

My girls had met at their school the daughters of a local Racehorse Trainer called Robert Alner. He was himself a hugely respected champion amateur jockey, and his girls helped mine with their pony difficulties. It was suggested that I might like to ride out with Robert one morning. Now at this stage I was still a learning aged student of riding, and this was a bit above my level I thought. Still, nothing ventured, nothing gained, so I turned up at the stables at some unearthly hour in the morning to ride a proper racehorse. Boozer had been a racehorse, of course, but he was in his dotage now, and these animals were in their prime. Being almost forty now, and having the right kit, I guess I did look the part to the other young riders in the stables, but really I knew nothing. I was led to one of the "quiet" horses in his stable and saddled him up feeling I had made some progress in this equestrian business. We set off and soon began to canter the horses, third gear and moving along nicely. I was proud that I had learnt at the riding school to perform a sitting canter, with my bum permanently in the saddle, and bounded along contentedly. That is not the way to ride a racehorse. "What the bloody hell do you think you are doing? Get your arse in the air." Another piece of friendly advice from the horsey world. But I loved it. Being amongst a string of horses in the early morning, riding from the Blackmoor Vale up to the hills and exercising these lovely animals was both a pleasure and a privilege.

I rode out with Robert and his wife Sally, for twenty two years. It was always in the early morning, before work, and gave me a wonderful start to the day. The stables went from strength to strength, and Robert soon became a professional trainer. "We" won the Cheltenham Gold Cup, the pinnacle of jump racing, one year with a horse called Cool Dawn. I watched the race at home with Linda, and told her that the horse would probably lead early on but that it would fade at the end and be well beaten. It was not one of the favourites. Ridden by Andy Thornton, who I had got to know at the stables, the horse stayed in front to the end. The only thing to do was join the celebrations in the evening at Roberts' farm. I can't remember how I got home. I exercised the winner just before his retirement, and still boast that I have ridden a Gold Cup winner! Not bad for a nipper from Balham.

Horses are dangerous animals. Injuries are common, especially to the National Hunt jockeys, who expect to fall off more than one race in ten. They are brave men, and often ride with injuries which would not be tolerated by other sportsmen. It is an extension of the humour with which riding accidents are received. I was thrown off a horse called Huntsworth one morning when he was startled by a pheasant flying out of a hedge and the rider was not paying attention. He was a great big animal, and to get back on him I had to lower one stirrup and climb up a nearby gate. Just as I was again in the saddle, with only one stirrup, he reared and threw me onto the gate. Laughter from the rest of the riders. I landed on the left side of my chest and felt something crack. It hurt a lot, but one does not make a fuss in the horsey world so I got back on again and we made our way back to the stables. "Rog, you look very pale" was the only reassurance I had when we arrived. My fractured ribs and punctured lung healed quickly, and I was back riding the next week. Because Robert and Sally had become friends, I was given preferential treatment when I rode out. They now had up to eighty horses at the farm, and sometimes we schooled horses over fences. When I say "we" schooled horses, what I really mean is that I rode an experienced animal and led the proper jockeys over the jumps. Riding a good racehorse over a jump is flying through the air aided by unimaginable power when the animal takes off; an unforgettable experience and I understand why jockeys are so addicted. Andrew Thornton gave me good advice, and later a very raw young Irish lad called Daryl Jacob joined the staff. It has been a pleasure seeing the latter progress to being one of the top in the country and winning the Grand National. Happy days. Very sadly Robert broke his neck in a car accident and is now paralysed, but I still see him from time to time in Dorset, and he can still recall all my errors! I have not ridden in France, and fear the lovely animals I rode then have spoiled me for the future.

PIGS.

Pigs are my favourite farm animal. They are intelligent, but not too intelligent, clean, when allowed to be, and affectionate if given affection. My father apparently used to keep pigs in Clapham during the last war, but apart from that I had absolutely no knowledge of the animal when I came to the countryside. I had a friend who kept lots of animals on her smallholding, and she encouraged me to join the newly formed local Self Sufficiency Group. This was an interesting collection of local dropouts, usually with long hair and a beard, and not just the men. But they knew about animals, and vegetables and how to build a house out of straw bales. An interesting bunch, and they taught me a lot at our infrequent meetings. They did think it a bit strange that a relatively high earning professional should want to mess about like they did, but I explained that life is an adventurous journey and I admired the route they had taken. That did the trick, and soon after I was offered a brace of piglets. I made a run in the field for them, cadged an ancient pig arc from one of my farmers, and off we went in the family car to pick the little animals up from Horton. They were Wessex Saddlebacks, an ancient breed, interestingly from that strange area called Wessex which had confused me a few years beforehand. They are black and white and especially suited to the smallholder because they are hardy and live outside. Carrying a couple of squealing pigs in the back of the family Estate car is not to be recommended. My two girls were competent with rabbits and kittens, but piglets are a little more of a handful. I am not sure if the screams were louder from the animals or the children, but we managed to get them home and into their run, the piglets that is. The only problem with pigs is that they eat, well, like pigs. However much they are fed, it is never enough. We threw all the family waste into the troughs, and the bill for pignuts, the commercially used food, increased every week. Luckily I had another patient at Pimperne who milked her Guernsey cow and made cheese from the curds. The whey was wasted down the drain. For many weeks my rounds included a stop to pick up gallons of the fluid which the pigs found irresistible. They grew rapidly, especially when I found another source of free food for them.

At that time there was a dustmans' go slow. The local Refuse Disposal Department was in dispute, and instead of waste being collected once a week it was left for at least two weeks. Castleman House, a local Home for the Aged, had lots of waste food, and it was left to rot and become infested with maggots at the side of the road. My rounds now included stopping every other day to pick up relatively fresh food waste for my pigs. I knew there were rules about feeding pigs waste food, so we bought an old Burco Boiler from the local second hand market and all the waste was boiled for at least an hour before being fed to the pigs. They loved it, I was happy, and the staff at Castleman knew that they would have no festering food outside their premises. It is a fact of life that is something seems of benefit for everyone it has to be stopped. One day I answered the front door to find a very imposing ex policeman who identified himself as the Animal Food Inspector. He wanted to examine my food processing unit as he had been informed that I was illegally feeding food waste to my pigs! Someone must have snitched on me. I took him to the old Burco Boiler in the stables, and he was not impressed. Although no meat was included in the food I took, and he conceded that there was probably no danger to public health, rules were rules and had to be obeyed. He would not go ahead with prosecution if I stopped my waste feeding immediately. I was miffed, the pigs were miffed, and the staff at Castleman saw the maggots and flies return. Sometimes there is no reasoning in the world. I have to say that in France there are some silly laws, but the French have the common sense to ignore them and carry on regardless!

The two little pigs became two big pigs, and the time came for them to be slaughtered. Ruth Thorne at Fontmell Magna, had a small slaughterhouse, came and collected the beasts, and provided us with some lovely pork a few days later. It is amazing how many plastic sacs full of meat comes from two pigs, and we sold some to friends and tried to cure some of it for hams. I remember soaking the big legs in brine for weeks, and ending up with a mouldy and smelly lump of inedible flesh. The rest of the meat was lovely though, and I had fallen in love with pigs. The next time it would be a pig for breeding from.

Snowy Sparkle was another Saddleback. I bought her from a local pig farmer friend, Ian Morton, who lived just up the road. She was already almost fit for breeding, and was named by the girls. She grew rapidly, and became a pet, a bit like another dog. In fact she used to love playing with the Boxer, and they romped around together in her pen. Pigs have very powerful jaws though, and poor old Henry often came off worse. Ian told me she was ready to be mated. He didn't have a suitable boar, but I knew another patient, John Davies, a few miles away who had one and he would be happy for me to use him. The boar only had three legs, for a reason I have now forgotten, but the most vital part of his anatomy was intact and he was a proven stud animal. It would be no problem to take Snowy over in the old trailer. Or so I thought. There are many ways to move a pig, and none of them work very well. Snowy was very happy in her run, and did not want to leave it to meet a deformed animal who was going to do unknown things to her. She had become close to me, and liked to roll over and have her tummy tickled and be talked to. In fact it was a real pleasure to spend some time with Snowy in her little arc home and pass the time of day. She would follow me to the trailer and put her front feet on the ramp but would go no further, even with a trail of pig nuts leading her up. Pigs can be moved with a board either side and another in front of them, when they will walk backwards, and this worked well until the ramp was reached and then she would go no further. Linda used to make the most delicious Yorkshire Puddings. Sometimes we had so many that they would be left and given to Snowy. They were, without doubt, her favourite food, but were only a rare treat, and certainly not her staple diet. But after several failed attempts at getting her into the trailer, extreme measures needed to be taken. A special load of Yorkshire Puddings were made, and a line made of them every few feet up the ramp. Success at last, the pig made her way up, contentedly munching until she was secured within. She was not too keen on the tripod boar to begin with, but he did his job with calm efficiency, his corkscrew penis depositing the future progeny of my beloved Snowy without problems. At that time I had a very attractive lady Medical Student working with us and she thought the process was the most interesting thing she had seen in her stay. There is always a short wait to see if the fertilisation has been successful. It wasn't. Snowy came into season again and we would have to go through the same traumas to get her into the trailer. But something must have clicked with her, perhaps the experience was not as traumatic as we had supposed. On putting the trailer ramp down, and calling the pig over, she shot up the ramp like a greyhound after a rabbit. Well, perhaps not as quickly as that, but with a keenness that was totally unexpected. She eventually became pregnant after the third attempt.

I worried about her pregnancy; in pigs three months, three weeks and three days. I fed her well, probably too well, and she became huge. Birthing humans was part of my job, but pigs are different; it is not often a human has a dozen babies. I spent some hours in her arc, soothing her with a variety of melodies and gently rubbing her enlarging tummy. My friend Ian lent me a birthing pen, a contraption which is good for first time pig mums because it prevents them laying on the little ones, and gives good access if any intervention is needed. Her due date arrived. Snowy was in her pen, eating voraciously and looking very content. The day passed, and then the next day. As it happened we were giving a dinner party at the weekend, with a farmer and our local vet amongst the guests. After the delicious meal and copious wine I relayed my worries to the knowledgeable friends. We made our way to the very large animal, who must have been startled by our late night visit, but she submitted to examination in her own relaxed manner. I was pacing up and down like an expectant father, anxious for the learned verdict. I did not expect the supressed giggles; to me the matter was one of utter seriousness. "Your pig is not pregnant Rog, but she has certainly been well fed". My world collapsed, not only the wrong diagnosis, but ridicule in the farming world, and the news sure to spread locally. It was only a few days later that I was seeing a local lady in my ante natal clinic. We checked her dates, only a week or so to go, and as this was her third infant she was very relaxed about the forthcoming birth. Her huge abdomen was easily felt, and the babies' heartbeat good and strong. I love seeing ladies in this condition and although reassurance was not really required in this case, I asked her if she had any worries. She looked me straight in the eyes, without a smile, and asked "are you really sure I am pregnant, Doctor?" She then burst into uncontrolled laughter, and I thought she was going to produce on the couch. Stories pass quickly in the country.

Snowy Sparkle was sold. She had been untrue to me and misled me about her condition. But I still wanted to breed the animals, and so a Large White cross Saddleback was bought "in pig". The children had named the first pig, so it was for me to name the second. I called her "Barbara" after the mother in law. The latter took it as a complement, as well she might, as Barbara became the new love of my life. She didn't mess me about either, and produced eleven piglets at the due date. Pigs have a variable number of teats, and it is remarkable that they usually have enough for the family they produce. Each piglet has its' own teat and invariably goes to that one, and some seem to produce more milk than the others. So some piglets grow faster than the others and there is usually one little runt, smaller than the rest. But all her eleven grew well, we lost none, and they were soon running and playing in their enclosure. Barbara was a good mum, and although they can be very protective when feeding, she allowed me to pet her and tell her what a good job she was doing. Little piglets often have their teeth clipped and tails removed, to prevent injuring each other, but that really only applies to intense farming, and here in the open fields there was no need. Testicles are another matter however. The six males needed to be castrated, as they can become too aggressive if left entire. By this time I had become something of a castration expert, having done dogs, sheep, and one calf. Piglets are less easy to handle, and are not keen on losing the family jewels. Catching pigs is an art in itself, but castration is done within days so they are less mobile than later. There are lots of methods of retaining a piglet, one of the most popular being a section of car tyre nailed to a plank and the little animal held firmly by the tread. Even better is to work with an assistant, but there were no family volunteers, so it was down to me to do the job alone. There are, apparently, lots of ways to skin a cat, so there must be other ways to separate a piglet from its testicles. After long periods of thought, the sac method was devised. I put the six in an old thick sac and held it between my knees whilst sitting comfortably. The piglets seem to like being in the dark and were not too active. One by one they were pulled from the sac by the back legs, and the ballbag exposed with the animal gripped firmly between my knees. A NHS regulation stitch cutter is ideal for the job, a small and sharp blade in a sterile container, and with one little nick, each testicle could be grabbed and pulled out. Pulling the attaching vessels rather than cutting them stretches the blood vessels and virtually stops bleeding instantly. The whole operation was done in a matter of minutes and the slightly lighter piglets seemed none the worse when returned to Barbara. The dozen little testicles were ravenously devoured by the chickens. There were no cases of wound infection, and the surgeon was very pleased with himself. They grew rapidly and were great fun to watch. A public footpath runs through the field, and it was common to see walkers stop to admire the antics of the family. We eventually sold most of them but Ruth Thorne killed and butchered a couple which kept us with the most tasty pork for months. Pigs are known as dirty animals, but this is completely false. If they are given enough space they will always soil in one area of the run, and tend to keep their sleeping places clean and tidy. More than can be said for my children!

Pigs love apples and they also love mud. And if they have both they are as happy as pigs in muck. We had lots of excess apples one year, some of them a bit rotten, but still appetising for a growing animal. I fed them lots and lots of apples. Fermenting fruits produce alcohol, and we had very merry pigs, who would have sung songs if they were able to. And because it had been hot, we had flooded one part of their run as a muddy cooling down area. The sight of a family of drunken pigs and piglets rolling about in heaven is a sight for sore eyes. Wonderful.

The piglets were sold on when they were big enough, and Barbara went on to produce several more litters. I gave her to my pig farmer friend a year or two later, and he kept her with about twenty other sows in a big field on the side of Hambledon Hill. She seemed happy there with her new friends, but if our family visited Ian and his family she would instantly respond to being called and would run over from the herd to greet us. Pigs are lovely animals and rarely given the credit they deserve for their intellect. It saddens me to see them intensively farmed, but, like chickens, that is the price for having cheap meat.

SHEEP.

I have kept sheep on and off for over forty years now. Never in any great numbers, but enough to keep us amused, improve the pasture, and to provide meat. I don't enjoy killing the animals, which I do myself nowadays, but, if one is not vegetarian, I prefer to know where my meat has come from and that it has been well cared for. The older I become the closer I feel to becoming a non -meat eater, but the time has not arrived yet. And there is little that tastes better than home reared lamb.

Our first lambs arrived in Dorset from Jim Shepherd, the aptly named farmer who looked after a large farm at Tarrant Gunville. They were orphan lambs, and raised by our daughters Sarah and Clare on the bottle. Orphan lambs are sometimes accepted by another nursing mother if she has only one lamb, but she has to think that the additional animal is really her own. One way of doing this is to confine the mother in a crate so that she cannot prevent the orphan from feeding, and when the little lambs gut becomes full of the milk she has ingested, the excrement is recognised and the new feeder accepted. Another way, if a lamb has died, is to skin it and fix the fleece onto an orphan. Sometimes the mother will be fooled and feeding takes place normally. The skin is then removed in a day or two when feeding has been established. In my experience neither of the above has worked, and so the bottle is used instead. Orphan lamb food is easily bought from the local farm shop, and after some initial reluctance the lambs usually take voraciously to their new diet. And of course, little girls love feeding little lambs. They seemed to be raised almost exclusively in our large kitchen, warmed in front of the Aga, accompanied by the cats and the Boxer, and became part of the family. That was the problem; the animals were not part of a flock, and were not well educated by the other sheep. Because they had not had the protection given by colostrum, the clear pre-milk fluid produced by a lactating sheep in the first day or two, they did not have the natural resistance that normally raised animals do. On several occasions the little lambs grew well and were almost big enough to go into the field, they would die for no apparent reason. Sometimes they ate a poisonous plant from the garden, but usually they just seemed to lay down and die. Sheep are well known for that trait, but it was no comfort to heartbroken daughters. A few did survive however, and some went on to produce their own lambs.

Sheep are good for the pasture. With horses and cows, the ground is frequently churned up and becomes a muddy mess. Horses, in particular, can make a field "horse sick", meaning the turf is damaged and full of unwanted coarse grasses and weeds. The little feet of sheep, and their close grazing of the ground, tends to compensate for the damage, and as long as they are wormed regularly the terrain benefits enormously.

We kept Jacob sheep. They are a very ancient breed, named after Jacob of Biblical fame, who allegedly kept and bred kept them. They are black and white, have horns, and resemble the conformation of a goat rather than the fat sheep we have now grown accustomed to. Jacobs are a rare breed, smaller than the average, and have very thick fleeces which makes them look twice as big as they really are. They are good mothers, and often have multiple lambs. Twin lambs are usually no problem, but three usually means that one is left behind and forgotten about, and the fox eats it. Sheep have only two teats, so triplets are sometimes a difficult to feed, and one becomes the runt of the litter.

William was our ram. He was not a nice animal, and with huge handlebar horns was a danger to anyone who walked into his territory. Apart from attacking the digger when our pond was constructed, be disliked the car trailer and would attack that for no apparent reason. Later the boys thought it was great fun to annoy him, and would jump over the fence when he chased them, but he usually got his revenge. At one stage I thought he respected my position of authority and I used to pet him on the head and talk sensibly to him. He would seem calm and submissive and then suddenly swing his great horns into my knee and slink away with a smirk whilst I reeled in agony. I did hold a grudge against this seemingly dumb animal who always outwitted me and betrayed my confidence. My revenge came at shearing time.

Shearing sheep was another skill to be learned. Nowadays we have electric shearers which make the job easy; in those days it was done with hand shears I bought in Harts of Sturminster Newton. I still have them. We did not have U tube in those days so the books had to be consulted. John Seymours' "Self Sufficiency" was my bible, and he made it sound so easy. The animal is caught and sat on its bottom and the fleece cut off from side to side and then from the back. Fat chance. First the catching; easy if there is a trap, but we did not have one. The family and the dog, all seven of us, used to assemble and drive the animals into a little barn. It took a long time, with frequent escapes of sheep and sulks of chided children. Once caught, I had forgotten how strong sheep are, and they never seemed to settle and relax as John Seymour suggested. In the end I tied the animals' feet together and took my time and did it my way. The experts, with their machines, can fleece a sheep in a minute or two. My first animal took me one hour and twenty minutes! The shears were very sharp, and the operator very unadapt, and the poor first ewe had multiple little cuts through the skin. Wife Linda, the experienced nurse, dressed each wound with some antiseptic and a little Elastoplast, and at the end of the procedure the poor animal was not only semi -nude, but had little tufts of missed fleece in addition to multiple plasters. Not fit for the local show, and a possible case for prosecution by the authorities! My skill did improve with practice, and I could shear a sheep with the hand shears in about twenty minutes, fast enough when we only had a about half a dozen to do.

And finally it was William, the malevolent ram, remaining. He looked huge and fierce with his great fleece and huge horns, but the latter were a real help at shearing time. I could grab him, and with a great effort, turn him over onto his back by the horns and keep him still by keeping my feet on them. I am not usually a vengeful chap, but the sense of revenge in removing the great shaggy fleece and leaving a skinny animal, half his normal size, with his huge pendulous scrotum swinging between his legs as he sulked off down the field did leave me with a sense of justice done.

William was a good fertile ram. We had him as a youngster and he had not performed his duty until he came to us. To know whether the ram has performed, a stain can be put onto his chest so that when he has served the sheep, the evidence can be seen on its rump. I bought some "reddling", which is the red stain usually used in the past. Nowadays different colours are available and are used for different rams, and it amuses me to see how many colours appear on the back of sheep in some commercial flocks. William was adorned with his reddling on a pad which was fixed to his chest and we waited for the results with interest. Sheep come into season at slightly varying times, and a ram can "serve" several dozen in a flock. We only had six, and only one, obviously, had come into season. We deduced this because the poor animal was covered in the stain, not only where convention would have it, but also on the poor animals' side, head, and even its belly. I have no idea what antics William had been up to, but he had certainly been active. The other ewes were eventually served, latterly in a more conservative fashion, and we awaited lambing in the spring.

Lambing is usually done in special huts on the surrounding farms, but for us that was not practical. We did not know the exact days the lambs would be born, and anyway had no suitable accommodation for them. They always gave birth outside in the field. I am a great believer in letting nature take its course, and tried to leave them alone whenever possible. It was a highlight of our year to find a lamb or two that had been born overnight and who were contentedly suckling their mother the next morning. The little black and white lambs were delightful to watch as they bounded around the field playing with one another, and provided entertainment for the walkers and their families who wandered along our footpath to see them. But sometimes birthing was not so straightforward. One ewe died in trying to push out twins who had become entangled, and I was grateful to my chum Angus Campbell, who came and pulled the poor little dead animals out. Alas it was too much for the mother, who succumbed a day or two later. Ashamed of my lack of experience I dug a great pit to put her in and set fire to the corpse. The smell of roasting lamb which drifted over the village was greeted with delight until the cause was revealed. I filled in the pit, but the next morning it had been ravaged by the local badgers and there were bare sheep bones everywhere. Keeping sheep is not always fun. I became more adept at lambing over the years, but it was only rarely that assistance was required. Sheep do seem to die easily, and when I used to run around the countryside when marathon training, it was common to find a corpse or two on the sheep farms. We lost a few lambs to the fox, who would always take the weakling of a pair or triple; ewes can be very fierce and aggressive when protecting their offspring, but they cannot count more than one, and sometimes leave a baby unattended. We still keep a few sheep in France, where the fox is less of a problem, and one old ewe has raised her triplets for the second year running. Sheep are not stupid, just a little less intelligent than the other animals, and they keep grass looking good and are very tasty to eat. The children were informed very early on that the animals we kept were sometimes for eating, and accepted the concept well. Except daughter Clare that is. After we had killed one of the orphan lambs she had raised she refused to eat it and has not touched lamb since then. Even the smell of cooking lamb makes her uneasy. Have we permanently damaged our daughter? She is not a vegetarian so I think not!

THE FOX.

If any animal has benefitted from the last half century it must be the fox. He is now very common in the town as well as in the countryside, despite the futile effort of the Foxhunt. I really do love to see him, often magnificent in his reddish coat and with his loping gait. But I don't mind him being killed either, they are a menace to the smallholder and we have lost innumerable duck, chickens, geese, and the odd lamb to Charley Fox. I do not understand why they kill all the poultry in a coop and only take one; it is said that the panic and the flapping about of the birds is the cause, but I have had a dozen outdoor ducks killed who were not housed. I have seen a fox climb a tree, and seen him wandering down the main village street in daytime. He is a clever and unfathomable creature.

Friend Raymond lived in a lovely house a few miles across country from his workplace. On his return from work in the darkening evenings, in one of the quiet lanes, he often saw an impressive large dog fox sitting on a mound at the side of the road. Like me, he admired the animals although they were a pest to be controlled, and looked forward to seeing him. Each time the Hunt came through the area he was fearful that "his" fox would be killed. There would often be a delay of a day or two, but then the fox would eventually reappear on his mound, sitting proudly just before the road wound round a bend. But one week, the Hunt had been active and the fox did not reappear. It must have been caught, and Ray was saddened that he would no longer see his old friend. A week later, he passed the mound, now bare and deserted. He accelerated, angry at the Hunt for ridding him of an old pal, and screamed round the bend. There in the middle of the road was Charley Fox, sitting up proudly. Too late, Ray ran over the fox and killed it outright. Justice is sometimes not done.

I lost a goose to the fox one winter morning. Christine, our secretary, was first into work and saw the beast trying to drag the heavy bird off from the field. She opened a window and with the scary warning of "Shoo fox", the animal ran off and left the corpse behind. I knew that it would be back that evening and decided to trap and shoot Charley. Our garden was surrounded by a high wall, with the field the other side of it and the dead bird a little way the further on. Before dark, I attached a length of strong fishing line to the neck of the dead goose, led it over the wall, through the kitchen window, and attached it to an old pendulum type door bell. I loaded my shotgun, placed a ladder in the garden against the wall, and waited for nightfall. The clanging of the old bell would sound the alarm and it could be heard right through the house. Darkness was descending when Des Alner, our friend and neighbour, who was a local schoolteacher, turned up. He had had a very difficult day and wanted to retire to the Bakers Arms for a pint and a chat. That was what used to happen, a pint and a chat with a mate rather than an appointment with the psychologist. I couldn't refuse a pal, but explained my predicament and that it must be only one pint and then back to fox killing duties. It was not one pint. We reeled home later that evening, me rather worse for wear, to be greeted by a rather displeased wife. "What time of day do you call this?" was the familiar cry, "and by the way, that bloody bell of yours has been clanging for the last half hour". I stumbled outside with the trusty torch in one hand and the shotgun in the other. Climbing the ladder to look over the top of the wall was not easy, and in retrospect marginally dangerous with a loaded shotgun. I had stupidly not charged the torch; the usually powerful beam had been reduced to a dim glow. It was sufficient to reflect the eyes of the animals in the field, but not enough to see them clearly, and I could not see in which direction the fishing line was being pulled. At that time we had only five sheep. I could count six pairs of eyes looking back at me! One of them was surely that dastardly fox who had killed my lovely goose, but which one? Anger at the fox was tempered by realisation that my aim would be alcohol affected, and that I did not want to shoot a sheep. The ladder swayed as I tried to strain my eyes to see through the gloom; the shotgun wavered dangerously, the eyes looked back at me motionless. I could imagine Charley Fox thinking that as long as he stayed still the silly bugger with the gun would not shoot. He was right, I didn't shoot, but remember shouting insults at the animal who had made me look a fool. The dead goose was gone in the morning, and Charley must have smirked all through his enormous meal.

RATS.

Very few people like rats. The odd teenage girl perhaps, though mine preferred guinea pigs and gerbils. The latter two were a bit uninteresting from my angle, although I do remember the gerbils developing interesting growths on the limbs which we tried cutting off. But nobody in our family liked rats.

We lived in an old house with suspended wooden floors. This meant there was a space underneath which were a haven for out little furry friends. One of the large farms in the middle of the village was sold, and the very impressive brick built barns were converted to housing. Hordes of rats had lived for many years very happily and well contained within the farming environment, and finishing off any food left by the cows. When the buildings were emptied for conversion the rats had to find themselves new accommodation. Scouts were sent out from the community and word soon got back that Yew Hedge House would be a suitable venue. Columns of rats, with all their family possessions, made their way the few hundred metres to our home and set up their new community. Our house was smaller than the huge old barn, so several surrounding properties were commandeered as well. It is not a comforting feeling to find that your house has been taken over by large rats. I am not sure why we hate them so. Maybe it is the association with disease, perhaps their habits of gnawing anything, and maybe because they are very wary and intelligent, and not easily controlled. And of course they multiply so rapidly that we have visions of being totally overrun. The first sign of the infestation was noise at night. We were used to night time awakenings with the children, but for me to be wakened by pattering feet of inhuman kind was a new sensation. "It's only a little family of those cute little field mice which have come in for the winter" was my reassuring reply, but the truth was revealed to younger daughter Clare a few days later. My daughter had, and still has, a remarkable talent, like her mother, of being able to talk and talk and talk. Especially on the telephone, remembering that in those days we only had a land line with no mobile extension. She was immovably installed one evening in the telephone chair in our entrance hall, engaged no doubt in a very important and long winded conversation about nothing in particular. We had tried without success to curtail the vital call several times, but it ended precipitously. From a gap in between the carpet and the floorboards on the opposite side of the room a large rat appeared and ran alongside the skirting board. Calm conversation on the phone was interrupted by a scream which must have been heard throughout the village. A distraught teenager, trembling with anxiety, and for one precious moment almost lost for words, entered the kitchen shaking and pointing silently towards where the entrance of the beast had been made. I made my way to the hall to find a brace of rats scurrying away and down the hole they had come from. After that the phone was much less used, at least by the daughters, and, as usual, Dad was told to "do something!" After the initial commotion had calmed down the family discussed the situation over a very light supper. No, the rats will not come and attack you at night, and no they will not eat the animals, and yes they are frightened of us and will always run away. Calm gradually eased the panic, but there was no doubt that we had an infestation. After the initial sightings rats would appear in nearly every room of the house, and yes they did run away, but it was not pleasant having them share our home. The Ratman was called from the local council, and was a very helpful and knowledgeable chap. He laid poison under the floorboards and reassured us that all would be well. He did manage to rid us of the unwelcome guests, but poison kills animals but does not remove the corpses. What a pen and ink (stink) over the next few weeks! Dead and decaying rats are good for slimming regimes as appetites were blunted by the aroma for some time. We did at last have the home to ourselves again however.

But although the rats had left the house there were still a few in the surrounding buildings. Indeed if animals of any sort are kept it is inevitable to have a few of the unwelcome rodents about. One day I went to feed the horses in the stable. We kept the horse feed in a large thick plastic dustbin in the Farriers' room next door to the stables. On opening the lid of the feed, a large rat jumped out and scurried away. I jumped as well, but tried to remain calm. He did the same thing the next day, and so did I. A cunning plan was needed. I reckoned that as the level of the food went down there would come a point when the rat would not be able to jump high enough to get out of the feed bin and I could then kill the animal. Daily the level of the feed diminished, and at last the rat could no longer jump out and was trapped. I felt very clever, but how to kill the beast? There was no way I could beat it with a blunt instrument; it would jump about and never stay still. I thought about filling the bin with water, but what if it swam well and the rising level gave it an escape route? With my adrenaline mounting, a solution was found. I had an old air rifle in the workshop, and lots of ammunition; death would be immediate by pellet in the head. I had to fetch a chair to stand on above the bin in order to get a good aim, but the gun was primed and execution would be imminent and immediate. It was neither. Rats do not sit still in order to be shot, and despite waiting and waiting standing on the chair with the rifle primed, it would not rest for a moment. I had not executed an animal in cold blood like this before, and it was only one of Gods' creatures after all, and was it all justified? My inner turmoil and trembling hands did not aid my aim, but the process had to be completed and I fired. Missed! And the rat was given another burst of energy and ran even faster around the bottom of the now holed plastic bin. I shot again, and again. At last one pellet hit the animal and the running slowed down. Pleased that the end was in sight, but anxious that the deed had not been fully done, a dozen or so pellets were fired into the now motionless furry bundle. Blood seeped from the body and it was dead. Life was extinguished. I shook a little, but gained confidence and decided to throw the rat from the bin into the bushes by the field. I took it by the tail, still feeling shaky and mentally disturbed, and threw it hard as far as I could, symbolically ridding ourselves of this unwanted intruder. But I had made a grave error, and had not noticed that the animal had been shot, several times, through the tail. Rather than the corpse being slung into the bushes, it flew up in the air and landed fair and square on the top of my head! The mind is a mixture of emotions at times like that; panic that the spirit of the dead beast had come back to terrorise me for my murder, and panic that maybe it was not dead and was in attack mode. Certainly it was panic that made me stamp on the corpse repeatedly until my sanity returned. I don't like rats.

GOATS.

A Goat is a sheep with brains and attitude. They will eat anything apart from what you want them to eat. They are the Houdinis of the animal world and will plot their escapes relentlessly. They have a thing called character, which is alternately delightful and demanding. We obtained a goat which we called Heather. I can't remember where she came from, but after running our menagerie for several years animals just seem to appear, often donated when unwanted elsewhere. Heather was a female Toggenburg goat, black and white and with small horns. She was housed in the field with the sheep, and soon became great pals with Bruno, our Boxer. They would play together for hours, with the power of the Boxer matched by the crafty use of Heathers' horns. But she used to jump out of the field and visit the local gardens, which did not make us popular with our neighbours. And one day the caretaker of the Village Hall telephoned the surgery to request the Doctor to retrieve his goat as it had eaten all the roses from the border outside his prized building. She became well known and even well-liked by the majority who did not grow roses, and would often be petted when she went on our daily walks with the dog. Heather loved wandering over Hambledon Hill, and often surprised other walkers when she came up to say "hello and have you got something for me to eat?" She was a little goat when we first had her, but grew rapidly. Her escaping became a social problem, and so we began to tether her. Tethering Heather was always a problem. I bought one of the corkscrew type anchors which twist into the ground, but she soon worked that one out, and would be found in the village with her rope and anchor in tow. More solid tying on points like a large tree worked better.

We decided to breed from Heather. She was now a mature young woman and needed a gentleman goat to visit. Whereas Rams and Bulls are commonplace, Billy goats, or Bucks are not so common. After asking again in the Surgery, after a few days we found a suitable animal. Eve Blanchard was the Solicitors' wife in Shillingstone, the neighbouring village. She was a well-known keeper of retired Greyhounds and multiple other animals. If anyone found a sick or injured animal in the area, wild or domesticated, it was taken to Eve for rest and rehabilitation. Her kitchen was never quiet, with a changing clientele of varied size and breed, and it must have been difficult to keep clean. When we visited to ask about the availability of Billy, she was nursing an injured Buzzard back to health, and it was having flying lessons in the house. Our conversation would be interrupted by this mini Eagle flapping above our heads and dropping little moist messages all around us. But she agreed that Billy needed some work to do, and he was apparently well practised. He was not a pure breed goat, but it didn't matter as long as he did his job. Heather came into season a few weeks later and we made a date for her visit to her Romeo. She was not a big goat, and the Horse Box seemed a bit too large for such a small beast, so I took her, with some wifely disapproval, in the back of Lindas' Estate car. The girls came with me, and we discussed the coming events on the way over to Eves' house. It can be summarised by saying that the mating of a goat is not a long and lingering romance. Heather was let out of the car into Eves' yard, Billy sniffed her rear end without even the merest introduction or foreplay, his act of insemination was over, in seconds. The girls wanted an instant replay like we see on television, but the performance was over and Bill went back to his grub as if he had been rudely interrupted. It was the first time I had seen a goat in reproductive action and even I was amazed, but Eve reassured me that this was normal. And to think I thought goats were intelligent!

The one talent of a male goat is to smell like a male goat. The odour of goat semen must be one of the most penetrative and persistent of unwanted characteristics in any animal. Our lovely Heather had been transformed from a neutrally odorous animal into a repulsive one. The girls wound the rear car windows down, and moaned loudly, Heather looked embarrassed in the back, and I was gulping fresh air from the side window. We arrived home and she was dumped into the middle of the field to share her new perfume with the sheep. But the smell remained in the car. Despite driving rapidly around the countryside with all windows and sunroof open my wifes' car still stank of Billy goat. I decided to say nothing to her and hoped the aroma would have dissipated by the following day. It did not, nor by the following week, and barely by the following month. I was not a popular goat keeper. No amount of spraying and cleaning could rid the car of the smell, and the children refused to use it, even walking sometimes to school. Never let a fertilised goat into your car.

But Heather did produce a lovely pair of twin kids, a boy and girl. She raised them well, and it even curtailed her escaping to some degree until she taught her offspring how to jump. They were weaned from their mother after a couple of months and were a nice diversion from the other animals. But we had too many beasts of all types now, and they had to go. Ruth Thorne butchered them for us and it was the first time we had eaten fresh goat meat. Very tender like all young animals, but with a texture a little different from the others. We were due to host a meeting with the other four Doctors in our Practise later in the week. This monthly occasion involved a slap up meal with lots of wine and banter and then an allegedly serious business meeting afterwards. The location rotated from one partners' house to another. Linda was a good cook and the meal was very well received. "That was lovely, but what was that tender meat we ate?" The reply that it was our baby goats was received with incredulity and some revulsion. People are strange; we eat meat, so what difference does it make which animal we slaughter?

Heather stayed with us for a year or two, and then I gave her away to a troupe of gipsies at Shaftesbury. Old Bob assured me he was going to breed from her again and I hope he did, but I guess that she, too, ended up in the pot. They are nice animals, but not for the beginner, and produce lots of good milk; our neighbour Des kept two for milking in a shed at the bottom of his little garden and told me that milking was such a relaxing pastime. Rather him than me.

THE COW.

We only had one cow. We called her Honey and she was a Guernsey. Almost all the cows we see nowadays are the black and white Friesians / Holsteins. But ours was a Channel Island breed known for their rich milk and gentle nature. The black and white animals are useful as they are bigger, produce more milk, and the male offspring are large enough to be used for meat production. When the little Guernsey or Jersey male calves are born they are often killed immediately because they will be worth nothing to the farmer. A sad waste of life. My friend, and expert builder, Gordon Northway, helped us on the smallholding and always wanted to milk a cow by hand. It seemed a good idea, and we bought a young female from the Millers at Fifehead, who were one of the few farmers milking Guernseys at that time. Like all the Channel Island breeds, she had great big dark eyes, and with her gentle nature was an immediate hit with the family. She grew rapidly and the time came when she needed to be mated in order to become a milking cow. The days of the farm bull looking after a herd of females was fast receding. It is far easier to impregnate a cow artificially, an operator inseminating the animal by inserting selected semen via a long tube called a "straw" into the cows' vagina. I looked after a couple of chaps whose job was to artificially inseminate cows for a living, and one of them offered to do the job for us.

Having a profession which involves little but putting ones hand and arm into a cows' rear end each and every day must have some satisfaction I guess, but I can't see any. I have no doubt that some sort of empathy with animals is essential, but after impregnating dozens of bovine patients daily, and meddling with the less than attractive rear end, what do they think about at night? And the task is not without risk. Apart from being kicked by angry female beasts I came across a condition that to my knowledge has not been written about in the Medical Press. Because of the depth of the cows' genital passage, and the fact that the vagina often clamps down on the inserted arm, the practitioners often had pain in the elbow. It was a little like Tennis Elbow, but often on both sides of the joint. In many cases it necessitated time off work, and time meant money to lots of the chaps, some of whom were self-employed. My intended paper was to be called "Artificial Inseminators' Elbow". Needless to say, I never got round to writing it and the world has been deprived of a vital observation of work related medical conditions.

Arthur came and expertly inserted the semen from a Hereford Bull into Daisy. She was relaxed and seemingly unconcerned about this major change to her future life, and munched her hay whilst the procedure took place. A cows' pregnancy is a few days longer than a humans' and we watched her grow steadily over the months. There is something very soothing about talking to animals, and a cow is a good listener, better than the restless pig or dog or horse. Honey loved to munch her food and listen to the troubles of the day, and seemed very happy with her enlarging waistline and forthcoming adventure. A lovely, very rotund and very Dorset retired farmer called Jack Bussell used to come and supervise Honeys' pregnancy. He never bought a stethoscope and never got her onto the scales, but assured us that everything was progressing nicely. One evening he arrived and solemnly told me that "that there coo gonna drop it tonight" I don't know how he knew, because she looked just the same to me, but he was right. By the morning labour was progressing well, but seemed to be delayed after a few hours. Under Jacks' supervision we attached ropes to the protruding little calf legs and with steady pulling from Gordon and I a pretty male calf was brought into the world. Honey accepted it with her usual calm, licked all the muck off and helped the little animal to its first drink. Animals don't cry and scream when they are born; I wonder why human babies do? Buster the calf grew well and was weaned from its mother after about six months, when it was eating grass and could cope without mothers' milk. He was bought by a fellow smallholder, and I knew he would be well cared for, but separating a calf from its mother is never a happy time, with the little animal pining loudly for hours on end. But Gordon could now start milking Honey. John Garrett, who had hand milked for years when he was a boy, came and gave us advice, but I was not really involved as much as Gordon. He loved it, and although his work as a builder was very time consuming he would always be there in the early morning and in the evening to milk the cow. And it meant that we had lots of fresh and creamy coverings for our cereals, albeit warm and sometimes with a bit of straw in it. I never worried about the milk not being pasteurised when it came from Honey, and the kids loved it.

Gordon milked Honey for months, but she eventually produced less and less, and rather than let her have another calf with us she was sold to a friend. We missed the fresh milk and the friendly nature of our lovely Guernsey cow. They are usually very placid animals, but protective of their young. This was demonstrated tragically to me when I was asked to visit a patient as an emergency one morning at Fifehead. She had taken her dog for a walk through a herd of cows and their calves. The dog was off the lead, was been bothering the young animals, and had been attacked by one of the mothers. Naturally my patient had tried to intervene and save her pet, but she herself was attacked and killed by a rampant cow. I shall never forget having to telephone her husband in London to tell him about the tragic accident. Cows are calm but dangerous when provoked.

CATS.

The feline world reigns supreme. Cats are far more intelligent than any animal, and a match for us humans. They are well cared for, have no control imposed upon them, and generally do as they please. I am ambivalent about cats, although we have had many in the past and have one now. It is difficult to justify having a bird killer that has no need to kill for food, especially as our birdlife is in decline, and the little vole and field mice corpses brought in as trophies are not eaten but left for us to clear up. But if a rat or troublesome house mouse is caught then the moggie is a hero. We always had a cat or two in the household. They are not a bother to look after and a calm purring pussy is nice to have on the sofa. What other animal is allowed on the sofa; these cats have us humans worked out!

Our first foray into the feline fraternity was when we were in temporary accommodation at the foot of the village. We were given a cat for the children, and they loved the new family addition. We did not know how old it was, but my astute anatomical knowledge identified it as a female. It ate well, and became bigger and bigger, then one night decided to move its accommodation to the hallway cupboard. In the morning the reason for the expanding waistline was evident six times over. The kittens were of all different colours, and of course the girls thought it was a wonderful event. Each little one was given a name, and they were the centre of attraction for our girls and all their friends. We knew that homes needed to be found for them, but that was no problem with all our contacts, and this was before we had a dog, so the little animals roamed freely in the bungalow and spent the night with their mother in the hall cupboard. One morning I heard a strange moaning sound from the cat. Luckily I was the first up that day, and found all the kittens dead in their bed. They had been bitten in the back of the neck, and the mother was distraught. So were the girls. I found out that the Tomcat will sometimes come back and kill its offspring so that the mother comes into season again. We had left the front door open, and he had obviously come in from there. Cats are cruel, but that is a human emotion that they probably would not recognise.

Once in Yew Hedge House, we obtained another cat which the girls called Meggie. She settled well with our first Boxer dog Henry, although she was always the boss. The sight of a little cat making a big muscular dog recoil with fear and respect is an intriguing spectacle. When the dog moved too close for comfort, a swipe with a clawed paw would inflict a painful and often bloody injury to the canines' nose. He soon learned, and once fear gave way to respect they lived happily together for years, often sharing the same bed. Meggie gave birth, on Firework night, one year, in Sarahs' wardrobe. Again we missed the actual birth, a pity because two of the kittens were left in the birth sac and did not survive. I guess all this birthing trauma was good instruction in the ways of the world, but again we were left with kittens that this time were difficult to find homes for. We kept two, one of which was a wild animal. I guess cats are like people with their relationships with others; most are gentle and relate to affection from us, but one of the kittens was uncontrollably aggressive and clawed and scratched anybody who went near it. We hoped the little thing would improve over time but it did not. A decision had to be made, and the animal would have to go. I made the decision, and I felt it was up to me to do the deed. I had never killed a cat before, and although it would be easy to shoot it with the shotgun, that would make a mess, and to drown the animal seemed too cruel. My colleague Jon Evans, was at that time the anaesthetist with me at Blandford Hospital, and we discussed the termination programme over an operating list one morning. The obvious answer was to use Thiopentone, a barbiturate anaesthetic used in small doses to send people to sleep, but which in large doses would be lethal. Control of drugs in those days was less restrictive, and I obtained some ampoules of the drug from the hospital. Like shooting the rat, it was not a pleasant experience, but one I had to do alone. The horrible cat was stuffed into a thick sac, which it seemed to quite enjoy, and I injected several times the human lethal dose into the beast. Cats seem to be very tolerant of human drugs, or perhaps the injection was not in the right place, because it seemed a very long time before the murderer had done his job. To my reassurance the family were all pleased the renegade animal had been dispatched.

I castrated the brother of the eliminated animal, but it did not stop him becoming a fighter with other cats. He often came limping into the kitchen with a variety of injuries, some of which needed treatment. The most memorable was a deep chest wound which became infected and a huge boil developed on the animals' chest. The time came that it was obvious the boil had to be lanced. Boils in every possible human location had become a minor speciality of my professional life, so an animal should present no problem. I was wrong, again. With the very reluctant assistance of the daughters, we wrapped the cat in several layers of towels so that it could not move any limb. The operating theatre was the kitchen table, but the animal had to be held still by several shaking hands to make the procedure possible. I stuck the knife deep into the offending pustular protuberance and liberated what seemed like a river of gushing, disgusting effluent. I have been on the receiving end of many nasty aromas during my professional life, but this one would have won the prize. My helpers recoiled, intoxicated by the overwhelming stink, and the poor animal wriggled free. He was the only one who felt improved by the procedure, and made a full and unremarkable recovery.

Meggie went on for years and years, as cats do. We had her sterilised, so no more kitten incidents, and she oversaw several Boxer dogs and educated each in her fashion. Eventually she grew old and a bit scruffy, and my daughters grew up and became less scruffy and more fashion aware. When Sarah returned from college in London one weekend she and Clare decided it was time to beautify the declining cat. She was shampooed, groomed, and I think her nails were painted. A long brushing and hair drying session was performed, but the cat did not look overtly grateful. Meggie died the next day, but she did look beautiful!

RABBITS.

I can vaguely remember the days before myxomatosis, when the fields at my grandparents' home in Bedfordshire seemed to be full of bouncing bunnies. Grandad was an expert at trapping them with a noose, and it supplemented their diet on a regular basis. After decimation by the disease they have gradually made a comeback, although the illness is still about. Bruno, my favourite Boxer, was, like the others, a useless hunter, but loved to chase the rabbits on Hambledon Hill, knowing that he would never succeed. We came across a poor bunny with the disease one day, and to his surprise the dog actually caught the blind and stumbling animal. Rather than be pleased with his conquest, the look of astonishment and sadness at the same time is a canine expression I will never forget. He let it go and sauntered off with a disappointed whimper, as if he had trapped an unworthy quarry. But children love rabbits, and so we had to have one. His name was Harvey, and he was a gift from one of the Staff Nurses at Blandford Hospital. I built a hutch which we kept at the back of the house, and it was with great excitement that we went to pick the little animal up. I have since learnt to be aware of free animal donations. Harvey was not a nice animal. Rather than wanting to be picked up and stroked, he much preferred to impart serious physical damage on my daughters. He would scratch and bite and kick the heartbroken carers. We did a rapid psychological assessment of the animal, who was a castrated male. Perhaps he had a grudge against the world for the loss of his masculinity, or perhaps he was having difficulty with his sexual orientation. Anyway we thought the purchase of a second rabbit was the solution. Blackie was female and settled in well, and even Harvey thought well of her and moderated his behaviour to some extent. The little girls could both groom their pets now, and all seemed well. Blackie did like to run off when let out of the cage however, but was easy to catch in the confines of the back kitchen. One morning there was a scream from one of the girls, a mixture of fear and excitement, when approaching the hutch. There were three animals rather than two! But instead of being an overnight and rapidly maturing baby rabbit, sired by a castrated male, it was a large rat. I am not sure if Sarah or the rat was the more frightened, but the four legged one had obviously broken into the hutch to get at the food, and had forgotten his port of entry. Dad was nervous too, but the rat went out through an opened door. So too did Blackie, out of the hutch, out of the kitchen and to freedom across the garden and into the field. There was no amount of calling and bribing with food that could get the black rabbit back, and we consoled the children with the promise of a Guinea Pig. We eventually forgot about Blackie. We did have lots of wild rabbits around Child Okeford, and one day a patient came in and asked if the black rabbit in the road outside was an escaped pet. This was several months after the escape, but Dad would be a real hero if he caught Blackie and returned him to foul tempered Harvey and the children. No way would the bloody rabbit let me within ten metres of it. No amount of calling "nice bunny bunny, here bunny bunny", nor tempting with food had any effect at all. It was only after what seemed like an age that Di, one of our receptionists noticed another black rabbit further down the road. Suddenly the truth dawned. The escaped animal had become friends with the wild rabbits and bred, well, like rabbits. After that the girls in reception became used to patients stopping their cars when passing the surgery to inform us of the black rabbit outside in the road. I certainly saw black rabbits in the village for several years after that, and wonder whether the offspring are still about.

POULTRY.

Chickens, Ducks, Guinea Fowl and Geese; all of them eat well, taste good, lay eggs and all make lots of mess. We still keep a few in France, but looking back there must have been many many dozen over the years.

Chickens are probably the easiest to keep. All they need is some corn to eat, a box to sleep and lay their eggs in, and some water to drink. All these fancy hutches are a waste of time and money, and I have never heard a chicken complain of poor accommodation. In Child Okeford there was a couple of battery farms, one raising many thousands of chickens for consumption, and another for egg production. When the little chicks are first brought into the large barn for raising they occupy a few square metres of the floor. After only six weeks in artificial light and intense feeding they are almost ready for slaughter and consumption, and they fill the barn completely. Some are lame, many die, but they satisfy our quest for cheap meat. Our chickens took about six months to become properly grown, and it was fun to see them pecking all the new buds out of our flowerbeds! The factory egg layers were cramped in little cages and their eggs fell through the holes in the floor to be collected automatically. After a year in the constant light they laid slightly less eggs and were sent to slaughter. The manure from both battery farms was emptied once a year and the flies and stink they caused was not pleasant.

The children enjoyed collecting our eggs and sometimes even managed to get them back into the house without breaking them. We ate lots of eggs; sometimes they had two yolks and were huge, and keenly fought for. We had all sorts of breeds, the pretty Maran, with its brown speckled eggs, and the Light Sussex that laid so well, to the nameless brownish birds so common nowadays. One of the highlights of the chicken year was when we were given two or three from the Battery farm when they were doing the annual clear out. The poor birds were almost featherless, had had their beaks clipped so that they did not damage each other, and had never seen the sky. Over the weeks they transformed into proper chickens, learning to scrape the earth for food and getting a good feathery coat. Often the first thing they did was to look upwards at the sky as if to say that the light bulb had changed. We felt proud that the poor birds had been given the chance of a proper life, and they rewarded us with lots of eggs for several years.

I was given five Bantam chicks one year. Bantams are the hooligans of the chicken world. They fly well, will fight with any other bird, although they are much smaller, and roam anywhere. It was pretty useless to keep them in the run unless I clipped their wings, a process which is a pain to do and only lasts for a couple of months anyway. We did not want them to be eaten by the fox, so had to find somewhere for the birds to live. The rafters in the horse stables seemed to be a good choice; it was high enough to be out of the way, and the cockerel amongst them would be less heard. The problem was that they did not want to fly up there and were content to sit on the wall between the horses. Each evening after dusk, when they were sleeping, we crept into the stables, pushed the horses aside, grabbed a bantam and threw it into the roof beams. Eventually they got fed up with the interruption of their sleep and flew up by themselves. Bantams are good breeders, especially when left alone; at the end of the year I counted thirty five birds from the initial five! They must have nested in the garden or the bushes around the field. I loved having them around, but the droppings onto the horses were not welcome, and most were given away.

We bred our other chickens and a cockerel is necessary for this progress. The problem with cockerels is that they make a lot of noise, especially in the early morning. Luckily we kept the first run in the garden, on the other side of the house to where we slept, so only the children were wakened at 4am. Raising chicks is easy; the mum does all the work and dad just looks proud, a bit like in our house. But the problem with chicks is that half of them are male, and cocks don't lay eggs. They taste good though, and so it fell to me to cull the excess males when they were big enough to eat. I had not killed chickens before, and John Seymours' book was again consulted. It looked easy, a pull and twist of the neck and the job was done; easier than chopping heads off. The first victim was easily caught, and held in the classical position under one arm, then the head grabbed in the other hand and stretched violently away from the body. Why do books make things look so easy? I pulled and pulled but the bird was still flapping desperately for what seemed like minutes. Eventually its neck seemed to be about twice as long as previously, and the job was done. I was sweating, partly with effort, and mainly with anxiety. I put the corpse on the compost heap and went into the house for a comforting cup of tea with the wife. We planned to do the plucking immediately whilst the body was still warm, so went straight back outside into the garden. But where was the dead bird? Nothing to be seen on the heap, and nothing nearby. We heard a muffled gurgling from the lawn area. A chicken could be seen running around in circles with its head hanging at a strange angle from its neck. It fell over a few times but was clearly not in the throes of imminent death. Trying to run around behind a circling chicken with a floppy head in the middle of the lawn must have been a comical sight for some, but for me it was the epitome of failed assassination, and I felt useless and cruel. Perhaps because of personal rage, when the bird was caught, the second attempt at neck dislocation resulted in the head being pulled right off. This was not how it happened with John Seymour, but the result was the same. I did get better at dispatching chickens, but that initial trauma will always be with me.

Chickens take about twenty one days to hatch their eggs, Ducks take Twenty eight or more, depending on the breed. We often had chickens which went broody, that is they stopped laying eggs and wanted to sit on them to hatch the chicks. Broody hens are not any use for egg production, so a lot of the modern breeds rarely want to sit. Our chickens often went broody. Ducks lay eggs, often as many as chickens, but are not as reliable mothers in captivity. We sometimes put a clutch of ducks eggs under a broody chicken. She usually looked a bit fed up into the fourth week of sitting, as it was longer than she was used to, but animals are stubborn things and hatching was usually successful. Initially, a chicken raising baby ducks is no problem; they both eat the same things, and a bowl of grain will satisfy either bird. But when mum tries to teach her young to scratch the ground is when the problems begin; Ducks don't do scratching, and mums get a bit frustrated. And the real difficulty is when the duckling see some water, and rather than just drinking decide to go for a swim; mum has a fit, and jumps and twitters obscenities at her offspring. Mothering is never easy, or so I'm told.

Ducks are fun. They don't need much water to be happy, just enough to swim in and mate in! We had mallard crosses, Indian Runners, and Muscovy ducks. The Runners are the comedians of the duck world and a joy to have around, I defy anyone not to laugh at their antics, and they lay good eggs. The stronger taste of duck eggs appeals to me, and I ate them in preference to the chickens' eggs. We sold a few in the Surgery as well, but were aware that ducks eggs have a porous shell and it is not rare for nasty germs to contaminate them. There was no point in poisoning my patients as I would have to deal with the consequent problems. The Muscovies are much bigger birds, and very intelligent. They are the complete opposite of the Runners, and waddle in a very stately fashion over their territory. But despite being big birds, they can fly very well. We had one who decided she liked to live in our little lake better than in the garden. It was about a couple of hundred metres down the bottom of the field, but if I shouted or whistled at feeding time, the bird would immediately fly up and arrive for its meal. We kept about a dozen, but one night failed to lock them in their house behind the surgery. I arrived next morning to find twelve heavy corpses, all killed by Charley Fox. Ducks are very messy animals, but if they have enough room they are a real pleasure.

Geese are a different kettle of fish! Big, aggressive, untrainable, and dangerous. We kept a few Emden-Toulouse crosses in the field for a year or so. I was keen to get them after meeting "Old Bill". I looked after Joseph, an old retired farmer in a now demolished house in Shillingstone. He lived alone, and was guarded by his goose. Bill the goose was better than dog for warning of any arrivals. He would sound his goosy bark as soon as anyone approached, and unless his owner arrived would flap his huge wings and hiss at any intruder. Apparently he hated women for some reason, and would jump on their backs and peck their heads. Joseph did not have any lady friends. Bill himself, however, had a partner, and she laid eggs which Joseph used to present me with. A goose egg takes ages to boil, and will feed a small family if they don't eat much. They taste between a duck and a chicken egg and are highly prized. Bill began to recognise me and my fear of entering the property diminished to the extent that I could actually kneel down and exchange pleasantries with the old bird. Joseph was distraught when the goose died, and I took its mate to live with us. We bought another three geese, one male and two females, and kept them with the other animals in the field.

The new Gander was very protective of his girls. He would run towards any intruder and scare them off, be they human or animal. Even the Boxer was put in his place by a sharp peck on the nose, and kept his distance. But he loved to be a clever goose, and often appeared calm and friendly. Our neighbour was a gentle and rather rotund lady who loved all animals. She would often enter the field to say hello to the assorted lambs and piglets, and forgot about the Gander. One day she was bending over to say hello to a young sheep and was suddenly airborne after a particularly nasty bite on the buttocks from the now aggressive bird. She never came into the field again. We were told that the gander would protect the geese from the fox, and indeed it appeared that way. When a nest was built and the goose laid its clutch of eggs he would patrol the area and woe betide any intruder. So it was with both sadness and surprise that we found the geese dead one morning, again savaged by the fox. Never underestimate the fox, and never trust a goose.

Keeping poultry is not difficult and we would not be without them. They run free in our orchard and garden in France now, and although there is the inevitable damage to the flower beds from time to time, and newly planted specimens are frequently uprooted, it is a small price to pay. The interrelationship between the birds is fascinating, and they all have their own characters. The cat was put in its place by a sharp peck to the nose when it was a kitten, and has had complete respect since then. The old dog, an Airedale, despite being a terrier, has learnt not to eat the birds, and they exist happily together, even sharing the food scraps that we throw out to them. They have learned that if the dog does chase them, it is best to sit down and let their bottoms be sniffed and then she will move on to more appealing attractions.

Life without animals seems unthinkable now. They are always pleased to see us, need care, which makes us feel better about ourselves, and some of them provide us with food, be it meat, milk or eggs. They help to keep the grass under control, and eat some of the unwanted foliage. The dogs take us for walks, which is good for the health of us both, and they listen without complaining to all of our moans. Much better than those nasty pills for mental health.

REFLECTIONS.

It is late March in France. I have just come back from an early morning walk with our new Airedale puppy. The morning is fresh and crisp and in full springtime sunshine. The swallows arrived in my workshop yesterday, and the cuckoo is calling from the woods. Early flowers, the cowslip, lungwort and the celandine adorn the roadside and the scent of another delightful day is in the air. I have checked on our young sheep Flossie, who is about to give birth. We hope she has a singleton to join the triplets,

Eenie, Meeni and Myni being competently raised by the old girl Rosemary. Not surprisingly we aim to call It Mo. All is well here.

Time has flown by, but I guess everybody feels the same later in life. The world has changed since my career began. The telephone was a big heavy plastic thing which sat on a desk, and computers barely existed. We used to talk to one another rather than watching a little screen; nothing makes me feel more dislocated from modern society than watching a family in a restaurant all looking at their mobile phones rather than each other. Miserable old bugger I am.

And what did we do before computers? I have to admit that the immediate availability of worldwide knowledge has made life more informed, and being able to find out if that little bird outside is a willow warbler or chiffchaff by listening to the calls on You Tube is a bonus. I have just been talking on Facetime to my daughter and her twins in England; nobody would have thought that possible when my career began. So communications are different and we are more easily connected, with each other and with information from the outside world.

I am not sure whether people have changed. We expect more from life I think, and new cars and bigger houses seem to be the main goals in many peoples' lives. Above all, attitudes seemed to have hardened and some things formerly regarded as a privilege are now regarded as expected. The medical services have come under fire increasingly over the years, and there is no doubt that my beloved NHS is under very great strain. The service has become more and more expensive, and the governmental purse is not always open for our demands. But Doctors have changed in their workstyle as well. Gone are the days of staying on call for days on end. I remember not seeing the outside of one hospital for two weeks when I started work, but everyone was in the same boat and it was just regarded as normal. The fun of working together and practising a new job rather than learning the theory was starting a new chapter in life. Money was never an issue. Doctors have the most powerful union in the country in the British Medical Association, and they usually win their fights with the government. Politicians sometimes become ill after all. So we were well paid, and the pension after forty years is very generous. Those luxury cruise ships are mostly filled with retired medics, probably still boring people about their careers!

General Practitioners used to work long hours. It was normal to stay on call all week, night and day, and sometimes for the weekends as well. All that has changed now and the service has become much less personal and intimate. The patient doctor relationship depends on consistency, and it is difficult to maintain if a different doctor is seen at each appointment. The village doctor knew each of his patients well, and they knew him well. When I first started in practise, Richard Hollick, who practised in nearby Sturminster Newton, was a hunting man, and was never available on Thursdays until the late evening; all his patients new it and saved up their problems for the open access next day. He, like many GPs' in Dorset, worked alone, and was covered by a colleague on an informal basis when the need arrived. The introduction of Group Practises changed working hours completely, with one doctor being on call for the group out of normal hours. Now it appears that one doctor can be on call for a huge area of the country at night, and even has a driver to take him to calls. How anyone can be in two places far apart at one time defeats me. I didn't like the new system and tried to stay aloof from my partners by remaining on call for my patients at night time. I knew that if someone phoned at night I would usually know about the problem, and could often deal with it without a visit, and a genuine night call only happened about once a month. The argument that doctors would be too tired the next day if they worked for twenty four hours without a break is nonsense, but it was well argued by our profession and they got their way. General Practice became a job rather than a way of life. It made me sad that I was one of the few who thought we were throwing away a precious facet of our occupation. I loved my job, but over the years various changes and restrictions resulted in GPs' becoming moulded by a one for all machine which tried make us all practise in exactly the same way. Individuality was not allowed, and rather than doing minor surgery and dealing with trauma locally, all cases were sent to hospital, which deprived the patient of local treatment and overloaded the Casualty departments. Much more could be done in house by GPs' and it would make a real difference to modern day problems. My thirty years would have been many more if the system had not changed, but I took the money and ran!

So why leave the lovely county of Dorset? Times change, and retirement is a huge change. My predecessor, Willie Wilson, worked singlehandedly in our old house until he was seventy seven, then moved into a new house in the village. His posse of ladies continued to look after him for several years until he died. I retired at sixty two. For me the National Health Service had changed completely since I first started working in 1970. I no longer loved it, and felt that if I could not work in the way I thought correct, then I would rather retire. My social life had changed as well, and after spending some time living in another very pretty village, Milton Abbas, my new wife and I decided to cut all ties with the old life and start a new one in France. She had always been a Francophile, spoke the language, and so a new life in France began.

I shall always treasure my time in the wonderful county of Dorset, with the delightful mix of community I was fortunate enough to serve. It was a wrench to leave the local characters, who I loved dearly, but my job had been done and it was time to move on. Fittingly, the last patient I saw, when I made the journey over to France in my little kit car, was Clive Smith. I knew the family well, and of Vic's two sons, Clive had been told at school, where he did not excel, that he would never make anything of his life and that he was useless. I was driving in the old, cold, draughty car towards Bournemouth in the early hours, reflecting on life in general. A big sports car coming in the other direction flashed me. Clive waved from his new red Ferrari, no doubt coming home from a club where he did his Elvis Presley impersonations as a side-line from his hugely successful business. Well done Clive, that made me very happy, and it was a lovely memory of leaving the county of my hugely enjoyable career.

INTRODUCTION.

The Blackmoor Vale is in north Dorset, one of the prettiest counties in England. It is a very rural, and still exhibits accents and phrases of years long ago. The local poet William Barnes wrote in the local dialect, and many of his successors use words that were new to me when I arrived in the area in the early seventies. I found it charming, if sometimes alarming, to be called "my lover" by mature country gentlemen, for example, but it all added to the joy of the area. I was fortunate to spend the majority of my career in those beautiful surroundings, and have tried to portray my journey to that part of the world and the amusing incidents that have happened along the way, involving people, pursuits and animals. I am told that I often described finished tasks as a "Super old Job", hence the title of this little book.

THE AUTHOR.

Roger Prior is a Townie, born and bred in London. He always had a lust for the countryside, and after qualifying in Medicine in his home town, and then spending some years travelling the world with the Royal Air Force, settled in Dorset, where he worked as a G.P. for over thirty years. He has absorbed the ways of country life and wallowed in country pursuits and enjoying his animals as well as working in a sometimes demanding, but always amusing, career. He now lounges in retirement in rural France.

ACKNOWLEDGEMENTS.

Many thanks for the cover photo to Ruby Peak Farms in Lostine Oregon USA.